Main

EVERYBODY'S BROTHER

EVERYBODY'S BROTHER

WITH BIG GIPP AND DAVID WILD

GRAND CENTRAL
PUBLISHING

NEW YORK   BOSTON

Grand Central Publishing
Hachette Book Group
237 Park Avenue
New York, NY 10017

www.HachetteBookGroup.com

Printed in the United States of America

RRD-C

First Edition: September 2013
10 9 8 7 6 5 4 3 2 1

Grand Central Publishing is a division of Hachette Book Group, Inc. The Grand Central Publishing name and logo is a trademark of Hachette Book Group, Inc.

The Hachette Speakers Bureau provides a wide range of authors for speaking events. To find out more, go to www.hachettespeakersbureau .com or call (866) 376-6591.

The publisher is not responsible for websites (or their content) that are not owned by the publisher.

Library of Congress LCCN: 2013942951

ISBN: 978-1-4555-1667-4 (standard hardcover edition)
ISBN: 978-1-4555-8140-5 (signed edition)

CONTENTS

CONTENTS

INTRODUCTION

The Chronicle of a Crazy Child Who Found His Voice

FAMILY AFFAIR

No matter what, I always understood family matters.

The story that you are about to read may sound something like a psychedelic fable. Yes, there's a very handsome hero. Sure, he might not look exactly like those handsome heroes in other fables, but trust me, this brother is dope all the same. In show business—just like in a treasured comic book—you come across no shortage of strange and frightening creatures. But in my secret and sometimes scary world, at least all of the creatures you meet are very colorful. And as the record shows, I truly love color.

As you shall soon see, in the epic journey that has been my life, there are good guys and bad guys, heroes and villains, beautiful princesses, shape-shifting mutants, and pretty much everything in between.

Along the way, some crazy shit happens in my fable, and at times it might seem like this is going to turn into some kind of grim fairy tale:

Parents die tragically.

A sensitive but magical child lives in the wilderness. Okay, it was actually in southwest Atlanta, but let me say that things could get pretty wild there too.

Valuable and shiny objects are stolen. I know this because I'm the one who stole most them.

Innocence is lost—early and often.

There are cliffhangers and frightening moments when it appears that all hope is lost. There are false endings too because the way I see it, this story isn't over, not by a long shot.

And there's the mind-blowing moment of divine intervention when our hero—the angry lost child—discovers that he has amazing superpowers, like he's some kind of mutant X-Man or maybe even an XXX-Man.

Bit by bit in this story, our hero learns to master the mystical, magical power in his own voice and travels the whole wide world to try to get lots of other people to feel that same power too. He meets superhuman mentors along the way, gods and goddesses from the realm of music who offer sage advice and grant him blessings. He battles scary monsters and clueless executives who try to stop him from achieving his goals and sharing his gift. Time and time again, our hero defies all the odds and keeps on keeping on.

In the end, our hero rises up to the top of the game and grabs all that is rightfully his—and maybe even a little more while he's at it.

There is much rejoicing in the land or, as you freaks out there may call it, partying in the clubs.

But for all the bad behavior—most of it by me, I confess—there's still a very strong moral at the end. Wait for it.

Now here's the best part: It may all sound like a fable, but make no mistake—this shit is real.

This book—or whatever more modern device you have so brilliantly chosen to be holding in your hot little hands right now—is, in comic book terms, my origin story. Looking back, I feel that just like many other supernatural characters you might have loved to read about, I had to create myself due to circumstances beyond my control. As you will see, I was born in a sort of chaos but was mystically transformed into a very real character who was fated to ultimately triumph. I renamed this unforgettable character "CeeLo Green," and trust me, you're going to love the guy—just like I do.

In fact, you probably already know a lot about CeeLo, the Indomitable Showman. He's everywhere these days, appearing on stages from Las Vegas to London and popping up on your TV screens in *The Voice*, and in all kinds of specials and guest spots from *Saturday Night Live* to *Anger Management*. But he still has some surprises in store for you.

And along the way you will also meet somebody you don't know: a kid who was born Thomas DeCarlo Burton—most everybody called him Carlo—and who grew up to work out his anger in dangerous and unhealthy ways. That's me too.

In the end—don't worry, this is not even a spoiler—music saves my life. And all through this supernatural tale there is a soundtrack of some of the best and funkiest music ever made. As far back as I can remember I had voices running through my head: James Brown, Jackie Wilson, the Reverend Al Green, Bill Withers. Those beautiful, badass voices I heard singing and speaking to me from an early age taught me everything that truly matters in this world. Eventually they helped me find my own voice.

That's why I'm so happy to write this book, to expose my roots, to confess to my crimes, and to let you know how this showman got over in the business, with women, and eventually with the whole world. As a rule I'm the kind of guy who likes retaining a little mystique, but now I want to show where I'm coming from, literally.

To tell this story right, I've decided I need a little help, so I'm going to call on Big Gipp—my brother from another mother, who knows me better than anybody. He's a couple of years older, but we grew up in the same time and place—southwest Atlanta, just when it was earning its reputation as Ground Zero of the Dirty South. We became part of Goodie Mob together, and he's still a very important part of my mob today. Gipp has a lot of knowledge about things, not all of it verifiable. In fact, we've given him the nickname "Minister of Misinformation." But when it comes to Atlanta, music, and me, Gipp is the authority. So from time to time, Gipp is going to weigh in from the sidelines with commentary and extra bonus stories told from his own perspective.

I'm calling this book *Everybody's Brother* because, in my own strange way, I'm the proverbial boy next door—if you just so happen to live in a very colorful and extremely sexy neighborhood. It's a way of saying there's a black sheep in every family, so we can all relate to each other... even if you feel like the black sheep or the underdog.

By finding my voice, I figured out how to live, and to live pretty well if I say so myself. Find your own voice in this world, and I truly believe that you can do the same thing, and do it your way. I write this book not just to celebrate my own voice and to revel in my own success story but to help encourage the next generation to listen closely to the voices in their own heads, so that maybe someday they can rise up and share their voices with the world too.

So listen up. This success story could be yours too.

May we all find our own voices and keep on rising together.

Big Gipp: My brother CeeLo Green is a genius, a jokester, and very much a gangster. That smile you see could turn into a frown. What he wants is respect, and then you'll feel his love.

In the early days I could see that CeeLo was raw; he never had schooling or any kind of thing, but he felt strongly about what he was singing and it just came through to the audience. Over the years CeeLo has taught himself self-control. But the first time I was onstage with CeeLo, I noticed something crazy about him. He could not stand if there was anybody out there not paying attention to the show and listening to what he was saying. It bugged him out. He hated it. I think CeeLo knew right then that he had something to say to the world and that the world damn well better listen up. He always said, "If you not *saying* anything, then what the hell you doin' up there?" CeeLo knew he had something to say and that his voice should be heard.

That's one of the reasons that CeeLo is as big all around the world as he is today.

He's a musical prodigy with a photographic memory. He's like a computer. He can mimic anything he's heard, hear anything and tell you where it came from.

A voice like his only comes around every thirty or forty years. That octave is very alluring to the ear. You use that voice and put something behind it, you can control the world, you know what I'm saying?

He hasn't changed much. The only thing that's changed is his audience.

EVERYBODY'S BROTHER

CHAPTER ONE

Gettin' Grown in the Dirty South

Hey
Little boy you're not allowed to stay
You have to evolve inevitably
And I've sure come a long way

The road up ahead is so unclear
Back slidin' down the bottom of beer
Nobody knew if I would make it here

Sweet music set me free
From the statistic that I started to be
I wish my mama was alive to see

The memories of pain have scarred
And when I fall it's usually hard
But I get up and keep followin' God

—*CeeLo Green, "Gettin' Grown"*

SUIT AND TIE
With my mother and sister, all dressed up
with somewhere to go.

My very first childhood memory is a haunting one—which may mean something significant right there. Go ahead and consult the psychiatrist or spiritual adviser of your choice for a second opinion about that. In this memory, I'm asleep as a little boy and possibly even sleeping like a baby when, for some strange reason, I wake up right in the middle of the night. I'm in my grandmother's house, where we were living at the time. I'd gone to bed early—which is definitely not my style anymore—and suddenly I'm awake, and it's so late that it seems like everyone else in the world was asleep. Everything all around me is quiet and still and enchanted in some strange and elusive way. Not for the last time in my life, I decide that the time has come to check things out for myself and explore the nightlife a little bit.

So I climb out of bed without permission—which is definitely still my style—and walk through my grandmother's living room. There are these two lamps with little crystal-looking chandeliers that make a tinkling sound if you walk past them hard enough. And now I am very aware of all these shimmering lights and that tinkling noise. It stops me in my tracks. The vibe in my grandmother's living room very quickly becomes tremendously surreal and thoroughly spooky.

But then, just when I would have become totally terrified by my after-hours surroundings and run back to my room for a taste of safety, I start hearing this fantastic noise, this deeply magical sound that seems to be speaking to me as if it was being broadcast from a whole other distant and previously unseen universe. This noise is very mysterious to me, but even more, it is alluring. As it turns out, somebody in the house had fallen asleep with "Strawberry Letter 23" by the Brothers Johnson still playing on the stereo—and allow me a shout out to Shuggie Otis, who did the original song. Even all these years later, I can still hear those sexy, wild lyrics ringing out in my head. (If you don't know what I'm talking about, Google the song and take a listen.)

Now imagine being a little boy, waking up and exploring a shimmering nighttime world for the very first time, and then hearing that psychedelic solo with all that fantastic phased-up reverb and futuristic funk. That song's groove was freaking me out and drawing me in all at the same time. I was frightened, I was turned on, and I was probably only two years old at the time. What I had heard that night in the shimmering light was no more and no less than the future—namely, my future.

See, boys and girls, that's the amazing thing about the world that we all live in—our Creator is so stylish. You couldn't write the things that happen in our world. But apparently He can write them, and He or She does it all the time. Thinking back on my first memory now, it's almost like my feet hit the ground to that beat, just in time to experience this visitation by the Good God of the Holy

Groove. And in a very real way, I've been trying my level best to follow that groove ever since.

At least in my mind, music spoke to me before anything or anyone else did. "Strawberry Letter 23" is an eerie and haunting song to me still, and I'm thankful that it transported me into this other universe where I would make my own way—and eventually my own home. In a funny but very real way, I'm still that child in the darkness chasing something he doesn't fully understand and trying his hardest to touch that "red magic satin" Shuggie Otis wrote about.

What else can any of us do but just keep on reaching to touch the red magic satin we can never quite touch?

Everybody knows that a fable worth telling takes place somewhere magical, mystical, scary yet wondrous too. We all love a good alternate universe, and the tale that I'm about to tell you is truly a journey into the supernatural. Like the greatest stories ever told, mine starts off in one of those strange yet somehow familiar places where horrible and amazing things can and do happen, all the time. I'm talking about somewhere that exists in our hearts and minds and on every map that's cool enough to make mention of a land known far and wide to heroes and villains alike by one name with three words: the Dirty South.

The Dirty South is as much a state of mind as a place, located in the hearts and minds and streets of Atlanta,

Georgia, my hometown. In the Dirty South you get humanity served up in every shade and variety, with every sort of behavior—and I mean the good the bad and the ugly—all coming together in a rich and colorful mix.

Southwest Atlanta, where I grew up, was a place where church was big on Sundays, and so were talent shows. The neighborhoods were sectioned off into zones divided by creeks, train tracks, and rock quarries, by lakes and ponds, but they often blurred together. Tough projects would be standing right next door to regular middle-class apartments and tree-lined suburban neighborhoods. There were haves and have-nots going to the same schools. You knew kids who went hungry, who had no one at home, some of them growing up mean. There was crime in the streets, particularly after the crack money starting flooding the neighborhoods in the mid-eighties. And there was no shortage of jails and prisons to hold you if you got caught. But in one sense, we all came up in a privileged way because no matter what your family had, growing up in the Dirty South you got to see greatness all around you all the time. Whatever challenges you were facing in your life, it was still fun to watch all the characters in town and to be there and be alive.

Atlanta has always been the cradle of Black Consciousness. It was home not only to Martin Luther King Jr. but to seminal cats like W.E.B. Du Bois, who taught at Atlanta University back at the turn of the twentieth century and wrote *The Souls of Black Folk*. I believe that, to this day, Atlanta is where the black soul feels most at home.

The red clay of Atlanta raised Andrew Young, Maynard H. Jackson, Hosea Williams, William Andrews, Gladys Knight, and the Bronner Brothers. Musical geniuses like Curtis Mayfield lived there. So did Hank Aaron, the Hall of Fame baseball legend. Hank lived in a house in my grandmother's neighborhood, and he's still there right now. Growing up, you saw all these figures from the Civil Rights era driving in your neighborhood and you went to school with their kids. You saw people like Andrew Young come to your high school and tell you that change can happen because they were part of a change that changed the world. So kids from Atlanta always had a feeling that whatever they wanted to do, they *could* do.

That's the way my mother came up. She was one of five children of Ruby Farrell, a nurse from Albany, Georgia, who spent twenty-five years married to Thomas Callaway, a disabled Air Force veteran. They moved to the Cascade part of Atlanta back in the early sixties, when it was still a predominantly white area. Even a blockade put up by the mayor couldn't keep the black folks of Atlanta from moving in and moving up, because the time had come. Before long, Cascade's leafy neighborhoods became the hub of Atlanta's black middle class, which was coming on fast, and a magnet for all those rich and famous people I was telling you about. All five Callaway kids got good educations and good jobs. I have an uncle who does architectural work for the railroad, another who's a chef; one aunt in marketing for Coca-Cola and another who's just shy of getting a Ph.D. in health care administration. All of them are movers and shakers, but my mom was definitely the moving-est (and sometimes the shakiest too). She just never could settle down anywhere, changing jobs and houses and apartments as fast as you could change a TV channel, until an accident later put an end to her restless ways.

My mother was born Sheila J. Callaway in 1956 and grew up an athletic, fair-skinned girl who always acted more mature than she really was. And she could never be told what to do—which sounds very familiar to me. When she was fourteen she married a man named Michael Burton. He was several years older, and that was her pattern— she always liked older men. Come to think of it, I've always liked older women, so maybe that's where that comes from. My sister, Shedonna, arrived in 1973, about the time Mom and her first husband split up.

Now, I don't remember any of this, of course. I wasn't even born yet, so I'm relying on what I heard as a child and what's been told to me since then. But my mom's interest in older men extended to a sharp-dressing Baptist minister who was crazy about her but unfortunately already married. That was my father. I was born on May 30, 1975, and christened Thomas DeCarlo Burton. I was named after my grandfather, who had recently passed, and was given the surname that my mother carried at the time. Nobody knows where the DeCarlo comes from, my mom just liked the sound of it. She called me Carlo.

Shedonna remembers my real father better than I do, because he died of a heart attack when I was two years old. Even though he didn't marry my mother, I know he acknowledged me as his son, and I've been told he would always be visiting us wherever we lived. Our mom was already moving around quite a lot by then, at least three different places before I was three. Shedonna says my father wore his hair in long Jheri curls swept back on his head, and he sported the most stylish suits she'd ever seen a man wear. I don't remember that, but I remember other things, like his car. He drove a 1978 Seville that was black with red leather interior—which is not exactly red magic satin but just as nice. I close my eyes now and I can still see that Cadillac, even though I'm sorry to say I have a whole lot of trouble picturing the car's driver.

For some reason, I remember for sure that my father's cup holder was always full of peppermint candies. Putting those peppermints in the car is something that I've imitated many times in my life in many cars—maybe because it's one of the only family traditions that I actually share with a man who left this world so quickly on his way to the next stop. That and a love of fine clothes. I'm not kidding when I say that I was wearing suits to school in grade school, and carrying around the ivory pipe he left behind with my mother. It may not be the biggest inheritance any son ever received, but at least it's mine.

My dad also must have loved to put on cologne that smelled something like leather. There was a sort of manly, musky smell that I will forever associate with him. Yeah,

I know this may sound a little odd to say, but that's what stays with me about my father even after all these decades. I really only knew the man who was my father by smell. That's how I can remember him being there and then not being there.

There were always a few pictures of my father around somewhere wherever we lived. I wish I knew where those photos were now, but I really don't. Today, if I want to see what my father looked like, I just take a good look in the mirror. I'm told that I favor him strongly. But in an odd way, I've sometimes felt as if he almost never existed. For me, my father—and the whole idea of a father—became first and foremost a very big hole that I had to figure out how to fill somehow. I didn't always fill that hole with good things either.

Please understand that my earthly dad had the best excuse any absent father could ever have, but he left behind a void that could never truly be filled. Growing up all over the place with my mom, with my grandmother, my aunt, and my sister—and lots of times on my own—I was understandably pretty clueless about what it meant to be a man. Maybe because my father's voice was silenced forever, just as I was getting used to hearing it, I gravitated to another set of male voices, ones that I heard drifting into my earliest memories.

Big Gipp: Lo and I grew up in similar parts of town, but my life and his were totally different because my father was always there and sadly CeeLo's father was never there. My father worked for UPS and my parents were still married, and you could say I had a little better lifestyle than most of my friends. So my experience growing up was different and easier than CeeLo's. But CeeLo was far from the only kid living with that kind of void in his life.

We always had enough in our house, but where we grew up in Atlanta, you always had a friend nearby who didn't have what you had. We all walked the same streets. And we didn't feel inferior in any way. We learned the lessons of Dr. King, and we could go downtown and see where he spread the word. All of the Civil Rights leaders, all their families lived throughout our neighborhoods, so it was always about being someone who stood up for justice.

The black revolution started in Atlanta, and by the time we were aware, I think there were more black and white friendships and understanding than anywhere else in the South. My grandmother was a black country woman who never left the country, but she owned land so she could call her white congressman downtown and get him on the phone. There's still racism and there's still bigotry to a point, but

Atlanta was a place where if your people knew some people, they'd work with you. Yes, there were more white people in Atlanta who were rich, but there were plenty of rich black people in Atlanta too—there were examples everywhere that we could make it too. So there was no sense of hopelessness. We came up in that era when black folks started getting good jobs. Lots of families were moving on up. It was our version of the American dream—or something like it.

And that's the attitude CeeLo always had and the one that he got from his mother, rest her soul. His mom was an entrepreneur, a hustler who always had something going on, something starting up. She had a store in the mall, and so even if his family didn't have money, you would never perceive it that way because CeeLo has always had style—and his own style at that. CeeLo always had the freshest clothes. He always had the presentation of a street cat who was up on his game. Rich or poor or anywhere in between, he looked good.

I am pretty sure that I'm not the first man to hear voices in my head.

Some people hear voices telling them to do terrible things. Thankfully, I haven't heard too many of those voices lately. Instead, the most powerful voices in my head have always been those of older men who spoke to me and eventually helped me find my own voice. It wasn't just the Brothers Johnson on that enchanted psychedelic evening at my grandmother's house. I'm talking about musical giants like James Brown and Jackie Wilson—and all-time masters like Al Green, Bill Withers, and Ray Charles to name just a few. I'd hear them on the radio, or over at my aunt Audrey's, where I watched *Soul Train* every Saturday morning, and then sang along to the records she played while she cleaned the house.

Like my own father, some of these men were already dead and gone by the time I heard them singing, but somehow their timeless voices could still reach out and share their secrets with a little kid who needed all the clues he could find. Through those voices and their shining examples of what it means to be a man in this world, I learned everything I ever really needed to know about men, and women too.

Just like family members who knew and loved me, these voices inside my head became part of who I am today, and they all pointed me down a path at a time when I needed any sense of direction I could find.

To my ears, these great singers all sang in powerful and distinctive voices, and they all sounded like men living their lives on their own terms. Those men also represented the father I wanted, the daddy I didn't have. Somebody cool. I always thought, if I did have a daddy, this is how he would make me feel warm and cozy and totally interested in every word he was saying.

You can learn so much about a man from listening to his voice. I think back to the nimbleness I first heard in a voice like Jackie Wilson's—a voice so serious and so subtle and honey sweet, all at the same time. The very first record that ever spoke to me was by Jackie Wilson—it was called "Doggin' Around" and was a hit way back in 1960. Still, hearing it many years later, I remember being stunned by how this man was saying everything I wanted to say exactly like I wanted to say it. Jackie's song didn't say "fuck you," or even "forget you," like I eventually would, but in my head at least, the idea was pretty much the same.

Singers like Jackie Wilson had so much personality in their voices, and back then, they had to. Jackie was singing to the masses way before video killed the radio star. Back then you had to be able to establish your identity with just your voice. In the deeper voice of James Brown and ageless anthems like "I Got You (I Feel Good)," "Super Bad," and "Papa's Got a Brand New Bag," I learned so much about strength and about the unstoppable force of pure self-expression. From the gritty but always heartfelt voice of Bill Withers singing "Lean on Me," "Ain't No Sunshine," "Use Me," and "Grandma's Hands," I learned everything imaginable about character, and integrity, and how to be a man and still remain vulnerable to feeling things deeply. Something about the fatherly warmth in Bill Withers' voice helped me imagine that someday there really could be a "Lovely Day." I remember how much my mother loved that song, and I imagine how much she needed a "Lovely Day."

I remember the incredible feeling as a kid of not being able to tell where my voice ended and Jackie Wilson's or James Brown's began. I loved that. Singing along with those voices gave me so much more than simply a warm, comforting feeling—though Lord knows we all need that sense of safety sometimes. In the end, this was the best education that I could ever have, musically or otherwise. It was an education that spoke to me in a way that school somehow never seemed to do. See, I believe that you can't miss when you're learning from the greats—because this way you're learning your lessons directly from the best of the best.

Maybe that explains how, before very long, I could sing along to all of these amazing songs and imitate all of my heroes' vocal runs and turns, all of their dramatic stops and starts to a kind of exactness—to a point where my voice became flush right against theirs. Every time I sang along with these great singers, it was like I was hugging onto these voices for dear life—which in a way I suppose I was.

Without these voices, there would be no Goodie Mob, no Gnarls Barkley, and no CeeLo Green as you know and—I hope—love him. So when people come up to me today and tell me something in my voice reminds them of one of their favorite old soul singers, I have to laugh. In a way, they're just noticing a very strong family resemblance to all the singers who were like family to me.

As you shall see, from any perspective, I was a wild child growing up, and more than anything or anyone else, it was music and television that tamed me. I think my musical talent had to come from God—or maybe the other guy. My mother could sing, she was in the church choir, but she wasn't a singer. My aunt Audrey sang part time in a dance band that specialized in top 40s and R&B. But she's the only case of formal music talent I know of anywhere in my family. So I've always assumed my connection with music came from somewhere beyond just here.

Right before my father died, my mom got a job with the Atlanta fire department. It was such a big thing that she was written up in *Jet* magazine as one of the first seven African American women to join the department. There's a photo spread, including one of me and Shedonna with our mom outside the apartment where we were living then. My mom wasn't a big woman, but she was strong and smart and mentally tough. Again, I don't remember much about that time except that she was gone for days on end, because of her schedule at the firehouse. Shedonna and I spent a lot of time with Aunt Audrey or our grandmother.

Nobody knows for sure why, but my mom didn't stay with the fire department too long. It was a hard job for women, and she probably suffered a fair amount of harassment, although she could always speak her mind and stand her ground. She also never met a stranger, and she could be very funny. Aunt Audrey thinks she just wanted to do something different. So she quit that job and trained to be a respiratory therapist. She was also regional membership coordinator for the NAACP. There was nothing she couldn't do. My mother was truly a trip, and for better or worse, I was on that trip. Like a lot of moms in the Dirty South, she did whatever she needed to do to survive. She was always on the hustle, just to keep her family going. She owned a limousine service at one time, and she opened the first black bridal shop in the Greenbriar Mall, out on the West Side. I used to spend a lot of time hanging out there, checking out the styles in the shop windows. We may not have had much money, but I always knew how to dress.

All this time we lived in different neighborhoods. A lot of them. It was feast or famine, but maybe a little more famine, though I still ate more than my share. There were times when my mom would miraculously find some way to put a down payment on some big-ass house and we'd live there for a while then suddenly, when that jig was up, we'd have to leave in the middle of the night. We'd stay with friends for a while. Then we'd start losing those friends. Then we'd live in a boyfriend's house for a while. Then suddenly we'd be back in a big-ass house until we'd have to leave there too. It was crazy. We'd be driving in a Rolls-Royce one day, then be broke the next. Mom married two more times but never stayed married long.

The one thing that we could count on in our lives was our grandmother's house in Cascade Heights. We always felt welcome and safe there. Ruby Callaway Robinson—she remarried after her first husband passed—was a strong, old-school Southern woman with a heart of gold. Grandma worked for years at Fort McPherson over in East Point, then got her license as a practical nurse when she was in her forties. Thomas Callaway had been a terrible alcoholic, and she decided it was her mission to spread the word about the disease of addiction and give people the help she never got. She founded a grassroots campaign called CASCADE, Inc., which stood for Comprehensive Auxiliary for Southwest Community on Alcohol and Drug Education. She organized youth drug walks where thousands marched through the streets of Atlanta and set up all-night workshops where kids could spend the night safely. Her work got the attention of Nancy Reagan, who invited my grandmother to the White House and had her join in her "Just Say No" campaign. You could say this was kind of ironic, considering the kind of things I got up to when I was a teenager. But if Grandma knew, she never held it against me. I could do no wrong in her eyes. And it's always wonderful to have someone like that in your life. We were close right up until she passed away. Even into her eighties, she wanted to cook for me whenever I went back home.

I was raised by women and grew up an unusual, even peculiar child. I was extroverted on the outside but lonely on the inside. I always felt out of place in a way I couldn't explain. But I'm told I was an entertainer from the moment I could walk and talk. As my aunt Audrey remembers, "Some kind of way, Carlo was going to get somebody's attention." She thought I was an "old soul," but a mischievous one. One minute I'd be singing in an old-man's voice like Ray Charles, the next I'd be tying a towel around my neck for a cape, jumping off the furniture like Superman. Or faking an asthma attack, just to see what people would do. I went through a lot of phases, I'm told, and superheroes were my main theme. There was a time when I was the Incredible Hulk, and I'd take a scissors to all my clothes, shredding them the way the Hulk would do when he burst into action, and cutting off the bottoms of my shirts. I had another phase where I'd wear Spider-Man pajamas day and night, and sometimes pull pantyhose over my head for the best effect. But Superman was my favorite. I wouldn't take those pajamas off, even for school—unless I'd decided to wear a suit. My mother would try to talk me into wearing jeans or things that the other kids wore, but I refused. "Let him do it, Sheila," my grandmother would say. "He's just a child, so leave him alone."

While I was still being Superman, I also went through a break-dancing phase. I must have been in the third or fourth grade. I would take thick sheets of cardboard and tape them together, then invite the neighborhood kids wherever we were living at the time to come over and practice some b-boy moves. Now, you may have noticed that I've got a big head. Believe me, it looked even bigger when I was a kid, and I used to get teased about it. But it turned into an advantage when it came time to learn those head spins. There was another move called the centipede where you bounce on the ground like a worm. I got good at that too.

When my mother went shopping at the mall, I would dress up as Superman and go with her. Mom had found religion by then and didn't approve of secular music, but as soon as she would go into a store, I'd ask Shedonna to be the lookout while I slipped out and started breaking for tips. I'd tell her, "Just give me ten minutes and see how much money I can make!" A crowd would gather to watch the cute little Superman breaking, but as soon as I got the signal I'd scoop my coins and run. Mom would never know what happened.

My sister, Shedonna, was my protector and sometimes my accomplice. She wasn't so busy causing trouble like I was all the time, and she got labeled "the good child" because she learned how to stay out of Mom's way. We were always two very different people. She was more of an introvert, and me, well, I was more of a lovable psychopath. Shedonna had common sense, and I had none at all. But the two of us went through the same crazy childhood, and we're bonded forever. Looking back, I think the truth is that my sister tried to look out for her extremely troublesome little brother the best that she could under some very difficult circumstances.

There was a lot of love in our home, but growing up, Shedonna and I would argue over just about anything. I was short for my age, and people often thought we were twins, and maybe that just intensified the sibling rivalry. We always bickered about whose turn it was to do the chores. I used to drive her crazy when I stuffed my dirty clothes in the closet and ended up borrowing her clean socks to go to school. Yes, sometimes those socks had frilly ruffles, but I didn't care. I told you I was peculiar.

Even while we were torturing each other, there were still so many acts of kindness from my sister that I will never forget. For instance, growing up we didn't have much money, so when we got McDonald's, that was something very, very special. And I savored every bite, but as slowly as I ate, there would still come the moment when my Big Mac was gone. And I knew that however much we fought, my sister loved me because she would make the ultimate sacrifice—in my mind at least—and give me the last bite of her Big Mac. That, ladies and gentleman, is one definition of true love.

Shedonna was always a great student, but I never liked school. I thought it was kind of stupid, and I was always speaking my mind and getting in trouble. For the third grade we were bused to a mostly white school in Buckhead, one of Atlanta's fanciest neighborhoods. One day the teacher was lecturing us about George Washington and I raised my hand.

"Why can't we talk about Martin Luther King?" I said.

I guess the teacher wasn't used to being challenged by a little black kid, so she didn't have much of an answer. She said something about that's not what we were studying and that Martin Luther King didn't come from this neighborhood.

"Well, neither did George Washington!" I said.

The only good thing I remember about that class was that I met a kid my age named André Benjamin, who was also bused up from the Southwest. He would play a big role in my life later on, when I met him again in high school, and later as part of the Dungeon Family and a member of OutKast. But then he was just Dré, who used to get teased because his mother would smear Vaseline on his face every day before school. Teasing was something I already knew about.

There were many times growing up in the Dirty South when I wondered if the big mistake was not my father dying so young but me being born at all. My body was too short, my head was too big, I was strange and I dressed different, so I would get picked on. Sometimes I felt like I was just one big mistake. And there were people along the way who took one look at me and told me that I looked like a mistake too. For a long time, I didn't know if I had any purpose for being here. I looked different and I felt different.

I was always trying to test the theory that I was a mistake of some sort. You know the RCA dog they called Nipper, how he cocked his head and gave that quizzical look. As I got older, I could see people giving me that Nipper look from every direction. I got used to that look. It wasn't really hate—it was more like "he's peculiar." And I wasn't dumb—I could feel confusion from people then. I can feel it now. And I'm still just as determined as I ever was. And I still in an instant would protect and defend my right to be exactly who I am.

I know now that I am not a mistake, that I have a purpose and a gift from the Creator. But that's a big statement for me, and it took a long time for me to get there.

The truth is that just like the voices on the radio helped me find my voice, television taught me everything I ever really needed to know about the world. It gave me a vocabulary, it showed me how to talk to people. The way that I see it I have always been a bit like that strange, little blond girl staring at the TV set in *Poltergeist*. That little girl was me—and I look just like her too, don't I? All kidding aside, growing up TV was my favorite teacher, and too often it was my best friend as well. Television was shelter, and security, and solace—all of it broadcast straight into my home in color—wherever my home was at the moment. For me, TV always seemed supernatural and extraordinary, yet it was accessible to anyone who paid enough attention. Trust me, I've always paid full attention to the TV—unlike I did to the poor teachers at school.

They say we are all created equal. Well, we may all be equal in opportunity but we are not in ability, and for some reason, I have always had this odd—sometimes very odd—ability to focus. I was never much for the skill sets in reading, writing, or arithmetic. Those studies somehow left me cold. Yet there is a skill set to focusing too, and it's one I acquired early. First, I focused on those voices in my head. Next, I focused on how people acted on TV, and I tried to act and communicate like they did. I've always been a sponge—a big sponge soaking up everything that

I'm exposed to and somehow making it my own in the process. There have been many times in my life when I have come across as rude to the people around me just because my focus can get so intense when I'm watching or listening to something. I don't mean it that way. Please don't blame me for it—it's who I am. For better and for worse, I am a true product of pop culture.

In retrospect, I think a lot of people use television and the radio to shut life out, but as a child, I did precisely the opposite. For me, music and then television were my windows into what a better life could potentially sound or look like. Sometimes they were the only windows I could see through. I learned to speak well by watching the characters I loved on TV just as I learned how to sing from all the men on the radio. But what I learned from the songs I heard and the shows I watched went way beyond that. They taught me about walking and talking—the rhythm of life, which if you think about it is very percussive. Everything I heard on the radio and saw on TV became the music of my mind that I'm still listening to closely. I'm always thinking in circles and patterns, and cursive calligraphy. I always see these beautiful things in my mind— like my life is one long-running TV show with a fiercely moving theme song that I'm still writing.

I love great TV theme songs. I especially loved the *Soap* theme, and of course there were more famous theme songs like *Sanford & Son*'s, for which the all-time genius Quincy Jones was responsible. I just found out recently that Quincy did *Ironside* too—and I loved that one. Not long ago, I was talking about great TV shows with my country *Voice* buddy Blake Shelton and for some reason he asked me if I remembered *Benson*. I immediately began singing the theme song from memory because those old shows hit very deep with me. They weren't just sitcoms to me—they were life; they were an escape and an alternate reality that seemed a little more predictable and stable than my own.

Big Gipp: I grew up in neighborhood where Jean Carne lived. She was one of the biggest seventies' stars. In Atlanta in that time, you had Gladys Knight, Jean Carne, Peabo Bryson, all these soul stars of the seventies. They would shop at the mall on Saturdays with no bodyguards, not like today. We saw all the wrestling stars too. We never thought of it as "us" and "them." It was "we," all mixed together. It helped with building the scene at the time.

In the eighties there were only a few record labels, and most music was local. We didn't really turn into a real music city until the nineties, when L.A. Reid and Babyface came to town. It changed the city, and the attitude of people who wanted to be in music. All of a sudden Whitney Houston showed up in Atlanta, and Bobby Brown was around. And now we were seeing actual stars and artists doing it— right now. So we felt like—hey, this is our time! We thought, we don't have to make music for the locals anymore, let's make music for everybody. All of us were coming up together—the girls in TLC lived down the street from me all their lives. Rico Wade stayed up the street. Dallas Austin was the first breakout star from Atlanta, leaving school at sixteen and moving to Los Angeles. It was like, *Yo!* We got actual people that we grew up with who are making actual waves in the music business! So it helped with us formulating who we wanted to be. Dallas came first, then came Jermaine Dupri. His father was a big rap promoter and brought Fresh Prince and some New York acts to Atlanta. So we saw the best. But because we were raised to think for ourselves, when our generation started making music, we never just followed what other artists were doing. I feel like it's where we come from that makes us go to the studio thinking we can change somebody's life.

My tastes in life and in music have always been unusually varied. In the beginning, I was introduced to music by the greats—by those soulful voices on the radio that became my first father figures. Then gradually, slowly but surely, I discovered the music of my own generation—all kinds of music. My uncle Ricky was an amateur DJ with a huge record collection. I would spend hours and hours over at his place, listening to the music and memorizing everything on the record labels and jackets—writers, producers, sidemen, everything. My knowledge became deep and encyclopedic—and ecumenical. Soon there were all sorts of other voices that spoke to me—like Prince, who blew my mind wide open then and still does every time I hear him. Or Michael Jackson, who worshipped Jackie Wilson and James Brown too, and had learned their lessons way before me and then created something all his own that will live forever. And don't even get me started talking about the genius of Stevie Wonder, Marvin Gaye, Bobby Womack, and Sly Stone. Then there were all the rockier voices that spoke to me too, like Mick Jagger singing "Miss You" with the Rolling Stones. I loved singing along with "Miss You" so much that when I think back, I'm pretty sure I must have been missing someone pretty badly myself. I also loved Boy George and Culture Club and Duran Duran—and we should never forget Kiss.

Kiss scared the shit out of me growing up, and you have to study and examine what scares you because it means that on some level it connects with you. So I was frightened, but I was locked in, because you couldn't miss them and you could never forget them. They created a sort of comic book version of rock and roll and that was right up my alley. I had a Kiss lunch box for a while. I also had a Bee Gees lunch box. I love the Bee Gees too. At the same exact time, I loved George Clinton too, and still do. I've always been drawn to artists who will go to extremes to spare your soul and blow the cobwebs out of your mind, the ones who change the game and redefine the rules. I am a student of that.

The first singles I ever acquired came into my hot little hands because my sister, Shedonna, bought them for me. I will always be grateful to her for buying me the ABC single "Look of Love," which came out in 1981. I really loved ABC—those were some funky British white boys making true "Lady Killer" music. Shedonna bought me "Wild Thing" by Tone Loc, and later "It Ain't Over 'til It's

Over" by Lenny Kravitz. I loved that song then and I still do now.

In the end, music helped save me, and Lord knows I was already needing some saving from an early age. She-donna remembers how my lifelong passion for music led me to shoplift early on. "As a kid growing up, Lo would always head to the magazine section at the grocery store and take all the *Right On!* magazines, or the *Jet* magazines or whatever publication that had some about music inside it," she remembers. "Anything that had to do with music, Lo wanted it, and he was going to get that magazine the best way he knew how, whether Mom was going to pay for it or not."

If the magazine had anything to do with secular music, Mom was definitely not going to buy it for me. When I was around four years old, our mother started getting serious about her religion. Our grandmother is a Methodist, and we went to church with her when we were staying there. But Mom liked a more fiery style of preaching and a more Pentecostal relationship with the Spirit. First we started going to Grace Covenant Baptist Church, where Mom—never one to do anything halfway—got herself ordained as a minister. She sang in the choir and made announcements. Sometimes she'd call for the offering when we needed money to pay the bills. She became friends with the pastor and his family, who used to baby-sit us. Every Friday night they'd come over for a supper of salmon croquettes and biscuits.

I used to love watching Mom preach, which she did

part time. But when she really got into the Spirit, it sometimes scared the mess out of me and Shedonna. We used to go to tent revivals, and Shedonna and I would huddle together when our mother got in the line for a special prayer. We were afraid she would catch the Holy Ghost and pass out. And then what would we do? She caught the Holy Ghost a lot at that Baptist Church. It scared me to see her flailing around like that, but it also gave me an opportunity for some mischief. Shedonna remembers at least two times when I'd fake the Holy Ghost and fall on the floor. My mother would not be amused.

A few years later we switched to a full gospel church called the Fellowship of Faith. They used to speak in tongues, which also scared the mess out of us. The first time we saw them gargling and jabbering and carrying on, Shedonna looked at me and said, "I mean, are these people crazy? What is this, voodoo?!" Whatever it was, we wanted no part of it, and we'd sneak out when we knew that part of the service was coming up. We'd sit in the car for a while then get back in place before church was over and Mom found us.

There were a lot of good things about church too. Most of it musical. Every Friday night we had to go to what's called "family enrichment" and then go to church very early every Sunday morning. To make it more fun, I started singing in the choir and doing Bible raps for the congregation. We learned all the books of the Bible from something called "Bible Break," which I quickly memorized. "Lo's gospel raps became a phenomenon at our church," Shedonna remembers. "So Lo could save souls even when his was in danger."

It turns out that Shedonna understood me pretty well—maybe better than I understood myself at the time. She knew that while I was singing like an angel at church, bad things were starting to happen out on the street. The devil was sitting on my shoulder, and there was a battle going on inside me for my very soul.

CHAPTER TWO

Crime and Punishment,

or Chickenhead Goes to Military School

Born into these crooked ways
I never even ask to come so now
I'm living in the days
I struggle and fight to stay alive
Hoping that one day I'd earn the chance
   to die
Pallbearer to this one, pallbearer to that
   one
Can't seem to get a grip 'cause, my palms
   is sweatin' ...

   —*Goodie Mob, "I Didn't Ask to Come"*

SCHOOL DAYS
*Here I am apparently doing some higher learning
while a student at Riverside Academy, a place that had
a big impact on my life in a short time.*

People called me "Chickenhead." Then they ran the other way.

Today, the world knows me as that sweet, soulful black guy on some hit TV show. But I haven't come this far in my life to have to bullshit anybody. I come to speak the truth—my truth. I may look as if I've always been a pussycat, like Purrfect, that pretty white creature you may have seen me stroking so lovingly and gently on *The Voice*. Please trust me, I haven't always been that way. Not even close. However you want to spell the word, I am rather far from perfect—and somewhere deep in the Atlanta police files, I no doubt have the juvenile record to prove it.

So here is a little taste of reality for you. Just like all the most interesting heroes in your finer comic books, the truth is that right from the beginning, I've always had a little villain deep inside me too. I'm kind of like Two-Face in reverse. Which is interesting, because I'm a Gemini, and two faces come naturally to me. Then and now, I try to embrace all sides of my own character, especially now that I seem to be living such a happy ending. They say that before you can get high, you've got to get low, and as a kid growing up in Atlanta, I got pretty low—and as you'll see, eventually I got pretty damn high too.

So let us then get real. Back in the day, before I became the lovable, ready-for-prime-time character who I am today, I was a damned effective little criminal—with the emphasis on damned. If you wanted to give me the benefit of a few doubts, the best that you could say for me was that growing up, I was sort of half angel and half devil. I may have been doing Bible raps and singing in the choir, but as soon as I got out on the streets, my more devilish half was definitely getting his due. For better or worse—mostly worse, I'm sure—doing bad things felt like second nature to me.

So at an age when other kids might be out selling lemonade, I stole my ass off. Looking back at it now, I'm trying to think what was going through my head. I'm not trying to make excuses for my bad behavior here, but maybe I felt as if life had already ripped me off by stealing my father away from me before I even got a chance to know him. Whatever it was that had been stolen from me early on, I couldn't wait to try to get myself a little payback.

I started out shoplifting, trying to be sophisticated, then regressed to just snatch and grab. I remember one time cutting school with friends—which we loved to do whenever possible—and taking the train to an Atlanta Braves game downtown. The mischief began with us just fooling around on the train and grabbing people's hats. Mind you, I was a criminal with some conscience, so I didn't bother old people, for instance. No, I liked to pick on people closer to my own age or a little older. Soon I moved on from grabbing hats to stealing starter jackets and shoes. It was a slightly more innocent time when all the rage was kids stealing Air Jordans. Truth be told, I'm not proud of this, but I made lots of people take off the shoes on their feet and hand them over. What I was accused of—and frankly, mostly guilty of—was what is sometimes called strong-arm robbery. I intimidated people into giving me whatever I wanted at that specific moment. These weren't crimes of passion—more like crimes of convenience. I wanted things, so I took things. From sneakers, I moved on to jewelry and anything else shiny that caught my eye. Thinking back, I was sort of like a shorter, younger version of that character Deebo from the movie *Friday* that starred Ice Cube and Chris Tucker. Yet I wasn't the star of any movie other than the one constantly running in my head. Instead, I was just some little neighborhood thug always making trouble in the streets.

In some strange way, I think a hero is really just a villain who's had a change of heart. I'm trying to be honest here, and not too cavalier, because in the end, most of my crimes may have been petty, legally speaking, but not to the innocent people who got robbed. Those poor people were probably truly scared and paid an emotional price for being threatened and taken advantage of by a street thug like me. For what it's worth—which is probably not nearly enough—I am sorry.

In my own weak defense, I hardly ever stole at gunpoint. The thing is that I didn't usually need a gun because people sensed somehow that I was not to be messed with. I guess I always came across like a bad kid who looked like he didn't have a lot to lose. In a way, I felt like I didn't.

Growing up the son of two preachers, I heard a lot about sin and salvation—and right away I was interested in the whole combo platter. The way I saw life, it was never as simple as good and bad—it was always good and evil in my world. I associate both good and evil with the Spirit, they seemed somehow Supreme to me. Growing up without a father figure, moving from place to place, being a highly impressionable child, I felt like I was an ideal dwelling for good and evil, so that both instincts kicked in powerfully at different times. I leaned more toward the evil back then. I've become measurably sweeter since then. But make no mistake, I still see the darkness and the light, and I understand both. It's like Walt Whitman wrote in a great poem called "Song of Myself": "I am large, I contain multitudes."

I've often said I was a kleptomaniac, a pyromaniac, and just plain maniac. One time I almost burned our house down. Mom had moved us into a house in College Park but the heat wasn't turned on yet, so I made a fire in the fireplace to keep warm. For some reason I decided it was a good idea to splash the fire with gasoline to keep it going, but then the flames jumped back into the gas can. I freaked out and threw the can into the fireplace, and the whole wall started going up. We got the fire put out, but the crazy thing was: I liked it. I liked watching that burst of flames, knowing I was the one who caused it.

Back then, my behavior seemed natural to me, almost involuntary, truly elementary. And it was all about having the power. If you could ask almost anyone if they had a superpower, say the power to be invisible, and what they would do with it, probably the first thing they would tell you would be something criminal. "Oh, I'd rob a bank." I never got around to robbing banks, but I did a lot of bad things with my power.

Early on in the inner city, you tend to become part of your surroundings. It was a lifestyle. And not everyone wants to be the star of that show. But I wanted to be something, and I wasn't afraid to take the bumps and the bruises to become it. I can quote Will Smith, who said that his initial attraction toward acting was because "I wanted to be somebody. In matter of fact, I wanted to be somebody else."

That was me too. But I wasn't acting.

Based on my own early experiences in the streets and trains of Atlanta, crime can pay and pay pretty well sometimes. But eventually it's going to end up costing you too. Did I ever get caught stealing? Hell, yes, I got caught sometimes, although I was never locked up for long. A couple of times I got banned from the mall for my antisocial behavior. Once when I was in seventh or eighth grade the police picked me up for stealing some sneakers and delivered me to my mother at her bridal shop. Man, she started whipping me so hard the police had to break it up. I guess they figured it would be more punishment to leave me with her than to haul my ass to jail.

Mom didn't believe in sparing the rod, and she had a belt at home with my name on it. She knew I was getting into trouble, and from an early age she would chase me around with that belt. Sometimes I'd try to lock myself in

Shedonna's room, but it was no use. She'd always get me. But the beatings didn't do any good. In the end it was me who decided to roll back my life of crime. Or at least try.

As you get older and move further up the crime food chain, you begin to question yourself, because the rush you feel becomes less even as the stakes get higher. For me, my criminal path was leading to some truly dangerous shit. We'd have these big outside fights—like the Valley Boys and the Pony Boys would meet in a big park, and just fight it out like boys sometimes do—gang crap on a grand scale like in that movie *The Warriors*. The way that I remember it, guns came in with the drugs and the big eighties crack epidemic. And then typically you had a gun because you assumed someone else there would have a gun too. That's a recipe for disaster. That's how it became a kind of arms war right in the streets. Actually, it was like an arms war all mixed up with a black fashion show. Of course, leave it to the urban community to make just about anything about fashion. So for instance, I remember you had to hold your gun sideways, because that was fashionable. I don't understand why we do that, but we do and with a lot of style.

Word tends to spread quickly in the streets—especially when you're a really strange-looking kid who doesn't fit in anywhere and fights every chance he gets. I was hanging with some heavy characters, much older than me, and I was starting to realize that I needed to stop myself from becoming some random crime statistic. And eventually my rep was so bad that I was pulled right out of the Atlanta public school system and told to go somewhere else—anywhere else. So where else does a kid who is trouble end up? That's right. If it's not jail, it's military school. And so I—the Thug Formerly Known as Chickenhead—somehow ended up entering the ninth grade at the Riverside Military Academy in Gainesville, Georgia.

Big Gipp: Atlanta called itself the City Too Busy to Hate, and that's true enough. But the Dirty South has its dark side. Everything that seemed clean, it was not what it appeared to be. If you knew the right people you could do anything you wanted. There were people who got money on one side of the street, people without money on the other. But we saw that people from both sides dibbled and dabbled in the underworld. From the police to the mayor to everybody. That's why it's called the Dirty South.

Along with the magnolia trees in Atlanta there's a history of thug life and enough prisons and jails to hold our bad guys and take the spillover from other states. Rice Street for the locals. Metro for the bad youth. Jackson for the grown-ups. And the Federal Pen right downtown for all the notorious criminals, political and otherwise. Marcus Garvey served time there, and so did Al Capone and some more recent mobsters from the Lucchese family. Cubans from the boatlift tried to burn the place down in the eighties. The eighties was a decade when Atlanta's kids grew up fast. And let's not forget, when we all were busy getting grown, Atlanta was not just our home—it was also home to the Atlanta Child Murders, which scared both whites and blacks who wanted their kids in by dark. The whole city was terrified.

Things calmed down a bit after they locked up Wayne Williams—the man and the myth. But then the whole game changed around 1984 to 1985 when I was going to middle school. That's when drugs first started really hitting the streets in Atlanta. Suddenly, the ghetto kids were showing up to school with better clothes than we had, and they always had lots of money stuffed in their pockets. We asked ourselves, what are these kids doing? They come from bad homes, but they have designer clothes and they're presenting better for the girls than we are. All of a sudden kids in eighth grade were showing up to school in cars—kids like Rico Wade, who went on to become the leader of Organized Noize. Rico drove his own car to middle school even though he wasn't old enough to drive then.

There were so many kids from rich families being drawn into trouble and then into crime. We all mixed it up in the streets. You had kids like Maynard Jackson's children who were known to fight and get in trouble. Andrew Young—his kid Bo Young, he *stayed* in trouble. Our friends were always a mix of kids who had and those who didn't have. The street element was so strong then it drew us all in. The lure of the street was so strong then that it was like playing football—the biggest game in town.

I had already started turning myself around a little bit. During the summer between eighth and ninth grades I took a good job on a construction crew, building some of those houses that were popping up all over Atlanta. I was making $9 and $10 an hour, which was exceptionally good money for someone that young. Now anything I wanted, shoes and starter jackets, I'd do it out of pocket. It felt good. I liked that feeling of independence. Amazingly, it was my idea to go to military school, and even more amazingly, I loved the joint. The Riverside Academy was an hour and some change north of Atlanta. But for me, this new place was a few worlds away from the streets where I had been so successfully wreaking havoc. The campus looked like an old-fashioned fortress with ramparts, high up on a hill. Cadets were marching around the parade ground in blue uniforms and garrison caps—I felt like I had landed in military Oz. They say that young people actually want rules, and I think that's true—even if some kids like me still take pleasure in then breaking those rules. I loved the attention, and all these new authority figures who seemed to care what I did. I went to the Riverside Academy's website the other day, and on the front page it reads "Focused Learners, Cultivated Leaders, Dedicated Brothers." Well, at least I was one very dedicated brother.

Even though military school made a better man of me, the place definitely did not make me an ideal, follow-orders kind of soldier. Now, I didn't mind wearing the uniforms. As you may have noticed, dressing up is one of my great pleasures, and I like that martial style. But there were other aspects of the experience that I did not adopt so easily. Like inspections. Inspection was when you stood by your bed in the barracks in the morning and evening and checked your shoes and your bed and your medals and stuff to make sure everything was clean and orderly. Then you would march by battalion up to meals in the mess hall. I can reveal this now because I'm out of the school and they can't discipline me, but I used to grab an extra blanket and sleep on top of it so I could just jump up in the morning and go. I never changed my bed or sheets or anything.

I also confess that my first experience with actual psychedelics was when I dropped acid with some other cadets a few months after I arrived at the academy. I have never been the type to do things in the right order—so somehow I ended up taking my first hit of acid before I even smoked a joint.

For the record, here's how it happened: I had a great friend at Riverside named Doberman who was one tough-ass white boy from Florida. Still, right from the start, Doberman was down with me. I figured out that Doberman was my friend when this other guy at school was fighting me and trying to hit me with his rifle, and unfortunately for me, I didn't have a rifle with which to hit him back. That's when I heard my new buddy Doberman say, "Hold everything right now. Wait one minute." I figured that Doberman was going to kick his ass for me. But instead of taking this kid's rifle away from him, Doberman gave me his own rifle and said, "Okay, now you two guys go for it." That was Doberman—very tough, but very, very fair.

There was another time when one of Doberman's cousins sent him some acid and he generously wanted to share. And why not, since we were brothers in arms, even though only I was technically a brother? I remember that back then the acid came in those funny little tabs with little images of Snoopy or Charlie Brown on them that made it look kind of cute and harmless. Clearly, I was a kid with extremely shaky judgment, so of course, I made a bad choice and took the acid. Kids, remember, never give in to peer pressure.

I thought I had picked the timing of this trip carefully. I thought wrong. After classes at Riverside, there were athletics—which could mean anything from playing football to doing fucking archery—which was not my thing even though some people might think I look a little bit like Cupid. After I came back from football that day, I got dressed in my uniform and decided to drop the acid right after passing evening inspection. I was thinking that the chemical reaction might make dinner more interesting or possibly even taste a little better.

For whatever reason, the acid didn't kick in until later, much later. After dinner, if you failed a class that week, you had to go to study hall—otherwise you could just be free to study in your room. Well, I had failed something that week, so I had to go to study hall. I sat there in study hall that night just waiting for the acid to kick in and make that experience more exciting. Still nothing. When I came back to my room after that, it was almost time for taps. Then *phooomph!* The barracks lights switched out for the night.

I still remember lying in bed in the darkness and telling my friends, "This shit is not working. It just must not work on black people." By now I began to think my trip had been cancelled, so I decided to say my nightly prayers. Growing up—and even now when I don't forget—I'm still big on saying my nightly prayers. So I closed my eyes to pray…and that's when the acid hit me. Hard. I started seeing things—big white dots and crazy colors and shapes. I screamed, "It's working! It's working!"

I'm sure everybody was so happy that I was tripping too, but they weren't saying anything, because we had to be really quiet. Which only freaked me out more. But they were all used to the insanity because, after all, they were a bunch of crazy white boys.

Okay, they weren't all crazy white boys. I also had a friend named Ayala from some exotic country. That night Ayala got high with us and snuck into our room—which was popular because I had this ghetto blaster boom box with eight-inch woofers all across the bottom and two tape decks in the corner. That boom box was massive and had great blinking lights all around the woofers. (I just know that boom box is in some Korean flea market right now and I want it back. Years later, I think I saw that same model—it might have been in the "Music" video by Madonna. I forgot to ask her about that at the Super Bowl. Maybe next time.)

So we locked the door behind Ayala and were all just sitting and staring at that blinking boom box. Then Ayala started having a bad trip and went back to his room to lie down. A few minutes later he came back and started kicking on the door shouting over and over that a green man was trying to get him. We opened the door, but thankfully, that green man was nowhere to be seen. When it became clear that poor Ayala was tripping even more than I was, that somehow that brought me back to Planet Earth and under control a little. I didn't want to see a friend being that scared. I also really didn't want to us all to get kicked out of school or court-martialed or killed—all of which always seemed like distinct possibilities when you're attending military school.

I looked into Ayala's eyes and tried to calm him down. I said, "Yo, what are you talking about green men? There's no green men here." But there was not any reasoning with Ayala at that point. So then I went the other way, and tried to quiet him down with a little brute military force. I said to Ayala, "If you don't shut the fuck up about this green man shit, I swear I'm going to hit you." Ayala took a deep breath and considered my threat for a moment. Then he looked at me and screamed, "Better you than the green man!" In his own trippy way, Ayala made an excellent point.

In every way, military school was a true education for me. Even though I'd known a lot of white kids, I'd never learned to live with them before, and I definitely loved this close brush with cultural diversity. They say it takes all kinds, and I like all kinds. I was going to class and doing pretty good. But this episode in my life had to end prematurely. I didn't realize until after I got to the school what a big expense it was for my mom to try to keep me there. It didn't take long before it hit me that she could only afford the one year, and even that was pushing things. But like a lot of those tough decisions that life makes for you, this is one that worked out for the best eventually.

I called my mom toward the end of the school year and told her, "Ma, I've got to come home." It wasn't just the money. I realized that my problem wasn't learning to behave at military school. My problem was behaving in my natural environment, in Atlanta, where the good guys weren't the only ones with guns. So I told my mother, "If I don't solve my problems back home, then they won't be solved at all." In retrospect, I think that was something pretty profound for a thirteen-year-old to say.

Like her son, my mom was a beautiful and strange bundle of contradictions. She was like both a father and an uncle. She could be really liberal, and sometimes a little absentee, but at the same time she was very tough too. My mother gave me enough credit to make up my own mind and enough freedom that I could have ended up getting myself killed. But on some deeper level that neither of us ever totally understood, she always seemed to trust me to make the right decision...eventually.

I think she just prayed that she'd still be around to see me make a man of myself.

CHAPTER THREE

The Very Fresh Prince of the Dirty South

I don't recall, ever graduatin' at all
Sometimes I feel I'm just a disappointment
    to y'all...
...I admit, I've done some dumb shit
And I'm probably gon do some mo'
You shouldn't hold that against me though
    (Why not?)
Why not? My music's all that I got
But some time must be ingested for this to be
    manifested.

—OutKast featuring Goodie Mob,
"Git Up, Git Out"

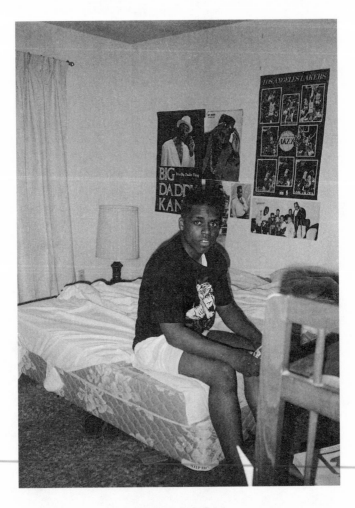

IN MY ROOM
Dig the expression on my face and the posters on the wall.
It all screams teen attitude.

When I came back home to Atlanta from military school at age thirteen, I stopped following orders entirely and started to freely pursue my own passions. And there was no shortage other new passions to pursue. For instance, having left an all-boys school, there were lots of girls to notice.

From an age that would shock many of you, I have loved women. Right from the start, being with a woman rubbed me the right way. Here's what I learned early—and continue to be reminded of often to this very day—there is nothing like the touch or the scent of a woman.

My first sexual experience was very, very early and with a much older woman. Today, she might be thrown in jail, but trust me, I would never be the one to press charges. See, one thing that you should know about me is that I always have admired older things. Older cars. Older singers. Older music. And yes, I always admired older women too.

I know it's rude to blow my own horn, but the truth is that I always had game with women because there was one thing that I could always do that woman loved—and that's talk. In my experience, the gift of gab will help you get a lot of great rides—with both fast cars and fast women too. That very first experience was with one of my mom's friends. How old was I at the time? Let me just put it this way—I was just a boy, but in her defense, I was already acting like some strange kind of man-child, wearing suits and carrying around that pipe of my dad's. So from an early age, I acted and behaved like a much older person, like an older man. To play amateur psychiatrist, I suppose I was dressing for a part that no one else was playing—the man of the house who wasn't anywhere to be found.

According to the textbooks, there is a clinical term that my mother was once diagnosed me with called pseudomaturity or some shit like that. It's a very real condition that causes young people to act like they are much older than they are. I was never tested for this condition, but I'm pretty sure I had a serious case of it anyway. It may explain why I grew up trying to charm the pants off my momma's friends. When I think back to the day, I remind myself of the smart hustling little boy in the movie *Fresh* who was always running the bags. If you've never seen that movie, then you must see it because I grew up a lot like that, only my unlikely story came to pass in the Dirty South and not Brooklyn. Actually, I was even more of a mix between that kid in *Fresh* and Damien from *The Omen*. I don't mean to say that I was demonic—Damien clearly had me beat in the pure evil category. But I always related to Damien in terms of understanding a lot at a very early age—and of course being devilishly charming.

I understood full well that my mother's friend was much older than me. Yet at the same time I understood that I could say the same thing twice, but a whole different way once my mother walked away. For example, there are two ways to say "Don't you look beautiful today." It all depended on how you savored that magical word "beautiful." And being as fresh as I was, I was going to let it be known that I was attracted to this woman out loud, but I instinctively knew how to communicate that thought and keep it between me and her in private.

That understanding of being seductive had a lot of impact, and even as a kid I was aware of it and used it to my advantage. Technically and legally, what my mother's friend did was wrong, but in my heart of hearts, I don't feel like I was a true victim. I was not a passive participant then—I could never be passive then or now. For better or worse, I always knew what I was doing at all times. And there tends to be something wickedly charming about knowing what you're doing, because it exempts you from being innocent. In a way, I'm not unlike that other devilishly appealing character Al Pacino played in *The Devil's Advocate*. It's like he says in that movie, "I'm the hand up Mona Lisa's skirt. They never see me comin'!"

Whether it matters or not to any judge, for whatever reasons, I was advanced sexually. And I'm *still* a lady-killer, but for some reason, some people I run across still don't believe me. They *still* don't see me comin'! The irony always tickles me because I know that I don't—and won't ever—look on the outside like the stud that I am on the inside.

My sister, Shedonna, also reminds me that my love of older women meant that I always had time to flirt with her friends. As Shedonna remembers, "Because we look a lot alike and I am only two years older, Lo would tell my friends that we were the same age or twins so that he could hit on them and date them if he could. When we were out somewhere, Lo was always explaining—'That's not my girlfriend—that's my sister,' and he'd be asking for numbers. Lo has always been what you would consider fresh—with a strong love for beautiful women. Lo's always loved mature women because he's such an old soul."

Maybe my attraction to older women had something to do with how different I was and how hard it was to get with girls my own age. I wasn't exactly the guy to date, I wasn't the high school football player. I had to get the girls alone. And if I could get the opportunity, they'd say, "Oh, I like him. He's cool."

That's what happens to this day. Maybe I've seen too much of life for the average woman. There's always that intimidation factor because I'm fearless. It's natural to fear what you don't know. And I make sure that you don't know me completely.

At the same time, when I was an adolescent, what the girls—and boys—*did* know about me probably struck real fear into their little hearts. Because Chickenhead was still around and making a comeback, just in a slightly altered state.

Having discovered in military school that taking acid was not my personal trip, right about then I started to smoke weed—a tremendous and pungent amount of weed. This aromatic if thoroughly illegal and unhealthy passion combined exceptionally well with my other recently acquired interest—hardcore rap of the dirty gangsta variety.

Like almost everyone else of my generation and the generations that followed, rap hit me where it counted. Rap altered my entire worldview. The first record that I ever bought for myself was when I got a job over the summer between eighth and ninth grades and I took some money I had actually earned and bought *Down by Law* by MC Shan. I loved that song and another song MC Shan did with TJ Swan on the same album called "Left Me Lonely." For reasons that may be obvious, I think I understood the meaning of being lonely from a very early age. Then I bought a 12-inch single for Public Enemy's "Rebel Without a Pause" which was altogether mind-blowing in its own revolutionary right, and on the B-side was another masterpiece that spoke to me—"My Uzi Weighs a Ton." The combination of brilliance and violence was so appealing to a young man and, compared to everything that came before it, so damn trippy. The "Look of Love," this wasn't.

For me and for countless others of my generation, Public Enemy's sound changed the way we experienced the world around us. This was more than political rap with lots of attitude. To my ears, this was like Parliament-Funkadelic for a whole new era—it was fantastically black and psychedelic and something about the group's mutant weirdness and desire to have their say really spoke to me. Public Enemy were true street poets and troublemakers in the best sense. This was rap. This was rock. And most of all, this was thoroughly mind-expanding.

The next rap artist to blow my mind was Too $hort—a little guy who had the big balls to put a dollar sign in his name way before Ke$ha tried the same thing. The music was minimal but with fierce beats I can still feel, and the filthy streetwise words left little or nothing to the imagination—a bluntness that helped fire up my own imagination forever more. Too $hort was talking about the street scene happening in Oakland, not Atlanta, but the same dirty things that were on my young mind were apparently on Too $hort's too. Looking back, some of Too $hort's lyrics make "Fuck You" look like an entirely sweet little nursery rhyme—in fact, the words "fuck" and "you" were two of the nicest in his songs. But as an immature, horny kid with a few anger issues of my own, I loved every word that Too $hort rapped, and just between us, I still do.

Believe me, songs like "Freaky Tales" by Too $hort were so trippy you could get a decent contact high simply from listening to them. I was too young to drive at the time, but this was music you had to listen to while driving the streets looking at girls. My friend Bert—we used to call him Super Bert P—he had a nice system with Cerwin Vega speakers pounding away in the back of his Hyundai Hatchback—and we loved going anywhere as long as we were listening to Too $hort tell everyone in the world "Fuck You" way before I did.

Other than the occasional crazy joint from 2 Live Crew, we had never heard anyone talk so vile, and we just loved it. This was music that spoke our language fluently. We were young wild boys out in the street getting drunk drinking Olde English—that's all we used to drink, 40s of Olde English. Rapping along with Too $hort, we could imagine that we were the ultimate gangstas. People think that music was West Coast shit completely—but it wasn't. That was some young stupid ghetto shit, and the good thing was that you could be stupid just about anywhere you wanted. Frankly, that might have been a pretty good rap name for me back then—Too $tupid.

The Atlanta public school system gave me another chance—perhaps unwisely—and I enrolled in Benjamin E. Mays High School to finish freshman year with all my homeboys. But I kept skipping class and getting kicked out for bad behavior, so I never moved up. After repeating the ninth grade twice, I ended up in Frank McClaren Technical School—a place of last resort for kids with problems or dropouts who needed to get their GEDs. That only lasted for a few months before I gave up for good. As you can imagine, this did not go down very well in my family full of professionals with advanced degrees. I hadn't told anybody I was flunking out and then dropping out. Shedonna, who was on her way to college at the time, was so disappointed she could barely speak to me. And, boys and girls out there, it is shameful not to get a formal education when you have the chance. I do not recommend the path I took. But by the time I left high school, I was putting myself through an intensive self-education in the School of Rap at the venerable University of Hip-Hop.

One of the only useful things about my time at McClaren was reconnecting with André Benjamin, my friend Dré from third grade, who had also turned into a bad boy. Dré was already rapping, and by then, so was I. We started hanging out together, and he introduced me to his friend Antwan Patton, who was going by "Big Boi." We'd go over to Big Boi's aunt's house and work on our rhymes. They were performing as a group called 2 Shades Deep at the time, and sometimes I would step in with them.

Many years later, once OutKast became an international sensation, Dré gave some interview in which he told the whole world that I was a bully in high school—which I wasn't. I only picked on bigger kids. But I remember that Dré called me something like "the Slap Master," which frankly I kind of like now that I think about it. As I always say, it's better to be the master than the slave. I remember hearing that Big Boi told everyone that I was a "high school hothead" who would "smack the shit out of people." Were they making all that shit up? Hell, no, but did they have to tell everybody? Seriously, I should slap those two again next time I see them. You know, not to hurt them because I love them both. No, if I slapped them it would just be for old time's sake.

It seems funny to me now, but back then, I was on the brink of something I was lucky to have survived.

I had meant to leave Chickenhead behind when I'd exiled myself to military school, but I have to admit that

I took a little bag of chickenheads to Riverside with me. I thought they might come in handy for something. And as soon as I got back to the neighborhood, I returned to my old, wicked ways—and then took it to another level. Sometimes, when I look back, I can't believe my infamous former self. Isn't it hard to believe, with what I've become? But the truth is the truth.

When I was young, I felt as if Evil wanted to put me in powerful positions. If I didn't turn out to be famous, I honestly think I would have ended up being infamous. By now, I'm pretty sure I would have had my very own special episode of *American Gangster*. And possibly, in my tortured soul, I would take just as much pride in that achievement. There's a certain pride in being good at anything. Even being good at being bad can be gratifying, whether we choose to admit it or not.

In a weird way, criminals are stars. There is probably not a rapper who doesn't consider Al Pacino in *Scarface* a true hip-hop icon, for instance. But at the same time, I've learned that being a criminal is the polar opposite—the flip side, if you will—to being a star. That's because when you have a big song on the radio or a big show on television—or in my case, both—everybody is suddenly more excited to see you.

Fame changes you only in the sense that it changes the way the world looks at you. I now know what it feels like to have people rushing toward you, wanting to get an autograph or grab a kiss or even take a handout. People just can't wait to connect with you on some level and share at least a moment in time, especially one they can capture on their cell phone and tweet. Being a thug was the other side of that feeling. Once I became known as a bad guy in the neighborhood, people were tucking their chains inside their shirts and literally were running in the opposite direction when they saw me, like I was a monster—which in a way I guess I was.

Long before I ever knew what it was like to be famous, I understood what it meant to be infamous. When I came around, people began to know what to expect, and I began to see them walk away as fast as possible in the opposite direction. They say that if you can't be loved, then you should try to be feared—and before long, I began to feel other people's fear most places I went. If stealing was my crazy, idiotic way of looking for love in all the wrong places, it definitely stopped working for me rather quickly.

Thinking back on the things I've done wrong, I've done some soul searching, and here's what I've found: To me, all goodness and evil come from the same place. I was willing to accept whatever was natural to me, and both ways were natural.

And so I was a self-fulfilling prophecy. I wanted to connect with people but could feel they had an attitude about me that I couldn't tolerate. As a teenager, people made me feel so alienated and awkward. If they looked at me funny because I was different, I just made myself *more* different. If they scorned me or disrespected me, I might want to hurt them. Sometimes I wanted to be a killer. I wish I wasn't serious, but I am. I think it was because I felt so much hurt at times, I wanted someone to hurt worse than I hurt, and that turned me mean and violent. I knew I had it inside me to love unconditionally, but I could never get over the fact that people could reject me without knowing me, before I could even introduce myself. In my confusion, I felt like that made people expendable. I felt there was something defective about the hearts of people who could hurt me that way. Going after them didn't feel wrong to me. It felt more like an extreme case of seeking justice in a universe where it could be elusive.

In my mind it went, "Now, I may be strange or peculiar and all those wonderful things that you call me. But let me take some initiative and show you why it's better to keep your mouth shut about me, or leave me alone." Not only would I give it to those who deserved it, I might get somebody who was looking the other way, who didn't have the balls to be disrespectful, but was probably thinking it too. I could feel it. This sense is what still helps me identify certain energies. My assumptions have protected me for a long, long time now. And ask me now, my knowledge of self shines so brightly, at this point I repel these kinds of personalities—they don't want nothing to do with me. My life is almost completely sucker free.

Thankfully, I eventually grew up a little and moved toward the light. Deep down, I think I really wanted to be loved more, not hated. That's finally what saved me and helped me put aside for good my fairly comfortable life of crime. That desire to be loved may be what ultimately saved me from killing somebody and in the process ruining my own life too. I began to realize that I actually did have a heart, and possibly I should start using it. Around this time I could feel a subtle shift happening in my soul—the Good was starting to edge out the Evil. I think it was because I wasn't just listening to music anymore, I was starting to create it. It was music that would finally give me the key I needed to connect with people. It gave me this benevolence. Who uses a word like benevolence? Certainly no black kid from Atlanta Georgia with an eighth-grade education. But it gave me peace, I understood. And my understanding began to outweigh my anger.

When I was about fourteen or fifteen, Shedonna started dating a DJ named Al, who was deep into the hip-hop scene. He let me tag along with him to the studio, where I got my first taste of how music is made. Here is where my sense of music history really helped me out as I found my way into the music business. I knew all about soul singing before I ever tried to rap. This is where all those voices in my head and on the radio from early on paid off for me. Unlike a lot of kids, I knew my Jackie Wilson before I learned my Too $hort. When I got into rap, I went deep. So I already knew that rapping and singing had been done by the Force MDs and by UTFO, but to the kids who didn't know, I must have seemed exotic. To some people, I still do.

My experience of hip-hop was expanding, and I was inspired by Grandmaster Melle Mel. Fusing the urban sensibility, urban urgency with social conscience—stylized on stage with spikes and leather. Melle Mel is truly the godfather to me. His theme song to *Beat Street* was prophetic, the best rap song ever. I studied the hip-hop masters Afrika Bambaataa and Soulsonic Force. Everything stemmed from them, they influenced the native tongue. They were putting out what hip-hop was supposed to be, a renaissance if you will of all the four facets of hip-hop: graffiti, DJ-ing, MC-ing, and, of course, dance. At the time, Queen Latifah also spoke to me, along with N.W.A., 8Ball, Heavy D, Biggie, the list goes on. But if there was anyone who helped shape my style, it was Tupac. I felt connected to Tupac's earlier approach, long raps like "Trapped" and "Brenda's Got a Baby." Storytelling was my forte when I started to write. I was carrying a rhyme pad with me everywhere I went, writing long story raps. The first song I ever wrote was called "Raiders of the Lost Rhyme." Too bad I don't remember the lyrics.

As stupid and stoned as I may have been back then, I already knew I wanted to be a rapper, but I felt I needed some safety in numbers. Having spent so much time in my young life on my own, it seemed like it was time for this lone wolf to get some kind of gang going for myself. Any kind of gang would do. At that moment, I could have met anyone in the world, and taken another bad turn and ended up dead. But instead I met a man who would help change my life—and who's still helping me change it right now—my man Gipp. In the movies they would say we met cute—I went over to his house to buy some weed. I was in the same class with his younger brother, so we knew each other by reputation alone: I knew Gipp was a rapper and he knew I was a robber. Eventually it was music that brought us together, and before long I had found my mob.

Big Gipp: Before I even knew CeeLo, I knew of him, because in the neighborhood, Chickenhead was infamous. He was not someone to be fucked with. Lots of good people were afraid of him. Hell, bad people were afraid of him too. CeeLo was always at Greenbriar Mall, and always with older kids. He was a known entity. If someone had done someone some wrong, the first person we were going to ask to slap somebody was Lo. CeeLo would be the smallest person there, and he'd walk right up and hit the biggest person there. He wasn't afraid of anything. I swear, back then Lo would walk up and fight a lion if someone asked him to.

CeeLo was a terror. He used to get on the train and do robberies hands on. He wasn't into having no gun, and he wanted no help. He just robbed people by himself most of the time—a lone wolf. And you've got to remember CeeLo was just this little guy, so at first, they didn't perceive any threat. So I guess you could say that those poor people were the first—but not the last—folks to go broke underestimating CeeLo! The people who didn't think he was a threat—well, that became one mistake in their lives that they would remember.

How far did CeeLo go? From my vantage point, he went exactly as far as you can go without actually murdering anybody. CeeLo walked right to that edge and then stepped back just in time. He was one of the young cats who were hanging with the big dogs. And the big dogs respected his game—like he was a top prospect they had their eyes on. The truth is that CeeLo probably could have done very well in a life of crime. But CeeLo stopped just short of becoming a lifer, and thankfully for me and a lot of other people, he ended up having a different life entirely.

So I knew of Lo and respected him from a safe distance. Then one night Lo came over to my house, and the very first words he ever said to me were "Yo, give me some weed!" That night we were cool, but CeeLo and I didn't say much to one another.

I never even knew he did music until one day I was over at a friend's house with my crew, Khujo and T-Mo. CeeLo showed up and he and Khujo started rap battling. In the middle of his freestyle, he started singing. And that was the first time I ever saw someone rap and then just burst into singing. I was like "Damn, that was incredible!" To see that kind of style from some kid from the South—it was amazing and got our attention right away. From that moment on CeeLo was in our crew, our family, one of us. He still is today and always will be, whatever else happens.

Right around this time, I found myself thrust into manhood in the worst possible way. One Sunday morning my mom was on her way to my grandmother's house to bring her some food after her hip surgery, when the van she was driving flipped over. They think she was reaching down to get something when she lost control. By the time the ambulance got her to the hospital, she was permanently paralyzed from the neck down.

There are some things in this life all of us would prefer not to ever remember, and this memory is the very worst of them for me. This was one of those real-life nightmares that started bad and somehow just kept getting worse. Mom spent the next three years in and out of hospitals and the Shepherd Center for spinal cord injuries. We couldn't afford to pay for nursing care, so my grandmother, who was a licensed nurse, took her in. She set up a hospital bed right in the living room and that's where Mom stayed. Like a small child, my mother was totally dependent on her own mother all over again. It must have been the worst kind of torture for such a strong and restless woman to be totally helpless. My mother had lived her life in a state of constant motion, never stopping too long to feel sorry for herself. And now she couldn't even lift a finger. Shedonna dropped out of college, where she had been studying nursing, to help out with her care. And I did what I could to pitch in.

As Shedonna remembers it, "When my mother was

injured, it was so tremendously difficult. Of course, our poor mother suffered unimaginably—as did our grandmother who took such good care of her. During that time, Lo was definitely the strong one between us. My mom had always tried to be everything to everybody—a go-getter, everyone's friend. So to see her like that in that position, in that state where she couldn't move, couldn't drive, and could barely talk, it was very horrible for her, and all of us too. But it was hard for all of us in different ways."

Again, my sister probably knew me better than I knew myself. She saw what was happening. "Lo was discovering music around that time in a serious way," she remembers. "I think that may have saved him and stopped his life from taking a very different turn. It became clear that Lo had real talent that could take him places. He was finally finding his path and his place in the world."

Among a certain select group of individuals in the greater Atlanta area, I was starting to get a reputation as a rapper who could sing. Using my voice to sing also allowed me to impress my family—maybe for the first time. It happened at my cousin Erica's wedding reception when I was about sixteen or seventeen. My mother was there in her wheelchair, along with my grandmother and everybody else in the family. I always loved gospel music, and as a kid I memorized every song that BeBe Winans ever recorded. So it seemed appropriate to ask to sing a sexy yet spiritual Winans song called "I Wanna Be the Only One" with Aunt Audrey and her band. We did it as a duet, and Shedonna assures me that I was electrifying. For once I became a kind of star—at least to my relatives.

Even though I was powerless to help my mother walk again or use her hands, I realized that what I could do was to share my voice on her behalf. I felt like I was meant to carry on for my mother, and I did not want to take such a privilege and such a duty in vain. I felt strong enough, and I was both willing and able. Having spent time in church, I wanted to be pleasing in the sight of my Maker and serving one master. It's easy to explain in retrospect because I'm older and I can only hope wiser. I did what I did because that's what came natural.

It's not easy for strong characters like my mother or me to feel helpless. And the way my mind works, I would never write a song about pure helplessness. I do not write songs to share that kind of pain. I write songs to empower myself and to empower other people who will ultimately have to face the inevitable and the unavoidable. Early on as a little boy, I learned that music is about rising above pain. It's about expressing your soul and touching the souls of other people too. That explains why, when the time came, I did not write a song called "Trapped" about my mother's suffering. Instead, I wrote a song called "Free."

Lord it's so hard livin this life;
A constant struggle each and every day.
Some wonder why
I'd rather die

Than to continue livin this way.
Many are blind
and cannot find the truth cuz no one seems to really
  know.
But I won't accept that this is how it's gonna be.
Devil you got to let me and my people go.
Cuz I wanna be free—
Completely free.
Lord won't you please come and save me.
Cuz I wanna be free—
Totally free.
I'm not gonna let this world worry me

We are all superheroes in our own stories—haunted by our pasts, yet focused on our futures. I was no exception. If my mother couldn't go anywhere now, well, then in my mind, that just meant that I was going to have to go everywhere. Even if my first stop was underground.

CHAPTER FOUR

Out of My Mind and into the Dungeon Family

In the Dungeon, I finally found my crew and I found my way in life too. In the Dungeon, I was set free in a manner that would open up the whole world to me.

GOODIE TIMES

Life with Goodie Mob was my education in music and life.

L ike the old saying goes, home is where the Dungeon is. For those of you who unwisely skipped your Introduction to Torture 101 course, a dungeon is a dark, forbidding, and often underground cell where prisoners are confined. Throughout history—fantasized and otherwise—dashing superheroes and nefarious villains like me have found themselves rightly or wrongly charged with unspeakable acts then thrown into a dungeon. As a rule, these captives cannot wait to make their big escape. But that's not how it works in my fable. In my very strange case, a dungeon turned out to be the perfect escape that I had been looking for all of my life. In fact, finding my rightful place in the Dungeon is what finally set me free.

While I was dabbling in psychedelics in military school, a group of very young hip-hop artists had been creating the sound of the Dirty South out of Lamonte's Beauty Supply shop in East Point, a gritty little city just south of the Atlanta line. Tionne "T-Boz" Watkins worked there before she became a big star in TLC, and so did Rico Wade, the teenage store manager and junior gangster who'd bought his own gold and black Honda Accord before he was old enough to drive. A lot of the young rappers in southwest Atlanta started hanging out in that shop, and eventually Rico and two of his homeboys, Ray Murray and Sleepy Brown, organized themselves into a groundbreaking production team called Organized Noize.

In the early nineties Organized Noize moved its headquarters to a small brick ranch house Rico rented for his mother over in Lakewood. There was a scene going on there day and night. Sometimes twelve, fifteen kids would be hanging in the living room and kitchen, drinking 40s and writing rhymes on notepads, having rap battles out in the driveway, or cramming into the studio in the basement, which wasn't even a real basement—it was more like a dug-out crawl space with red dirt walls. There wasn't room for much equipment, just an MPC drum machine, a keyboard, some recording gear, a table and chairs, and records all over the place. But what was going on down there was so good and so intoxicating that nobody ever wanted to leave. They were captives. So they started calling the place the Dungeon. And this cramped, thrown-together corner of the universe became the epicenter of a whole new rap scene.

Two guys from my neighborhood who hung out there—Jay Douglas and Killer B—brought me over to the Dungeon for the first time. It was definitely the craziest and coolest place I'd ever seen. That first night I rapped with Sleepy Brown and did some singing. He told me he liked my singing more than my rapping. Then Rico Wade walked in with André Benjamin and Antwan "Big Boi"

Patton, who were just starting to call themselves OutKast. Since Dré and I had known each other since third grade, he was excited to see me. "This is my homeboy we been telling you about," he told Rico. "Man do all the story raps. And he can sing!"

From then on, I was a member of the Dungeon Family. In the beginning, I would mostly just sit at the top of the stairs and try to size up the situation and figure out all of the players. The roots ran very deep there. Along with Dré and Big Boi, I already knew Big Gipp and "T-Mo" Barnett, who grew up in my neighborhood. They were slightly older than me, Original Gangsters—O.G. in the popular abbreviation—to be respected and possibly feared. Gipp was kind of quiet, but in an extremely striking way that let you know that he was someone special. Gipp was, is, and always shall be simply and utterly unique. Maybe that's why Gipp has always called himself—and in his heart of hearts considered himself to be—an earthbound mutant. I think maybe it's his ears. To me, Gipp is kind of like the black Spock—and just as lovable a character too.

Then there was T-Mo, who I've known the longest. T-Mo is four years older than me, but he is forever young. The man doesn't look any different to me than the day that I first met him—and that was back when I was in nursery school. Gipp was more or less a free agent, but T-Mo was in a group with Willie "Khujo" Knighton, another O.G. who was especially legendary on the streets of Atlanta. They were calling themselves Khujo and the P-Funk Goodie Mob. And that fit right into the spirit of the place, because the Dungeon Family was growing into a collective, a Dirty South version of George Clinton's psychedelic dynasty, a Parliament-Funkadelic of hip-hop. In the Dungeon, I finally found my crew and I found my way in life too. In the Dungeon, I was set free in a manner that would open up the whole world to me.

Big Gipp: Whatever it looked like to anyone else, the Dungeon was the center of the universe and heaven on Earth to us. We never really recorded in the Dungeon. Organized Noize would make beats and keep the beat on for two or three days at a time. You would go home, take a shower, go to school, go to work, come back, and that beat still be playing. And that's how we created songs. When we started to be able to record, we thought that we were on to something, we was big time. Outside of that, we'd just rap to each other and rap to the sky.

That was the first time I had a good chance to really watch CeeLo and figure him out. He was a fascinating guy even then. CeeLo was never the one rushing into a rap battle. Instead, he was always the one studying the music, sitting up against the drum machine and figuring out exactly how everything worked. Lo may not have paid much attention at school, but I'm telling you that no one ever paid more attention at the Dungeon. I guess in the end, that was the school he really needed. When he didn't know something, he asked questions constantly: How you do this? How you do that? He was never halfhearted. He was always focused on the music, while the rest of us were taking time off or playing the game. He never got into that stuff. He was always off listening to the music, and he was like a walking encyclopedia of music. He wasn't just listening to a song, he was studying who wrote it, who produced it. The rest of us were mostly just noticing what people were wearing on the cover. He always took a deeper approach. He knew who played bass. I know what sounds good to me. But he knew *why* it sounded good. It dawned on me later that back right in his first days at the Dungeon, CeeLo was already developing the talents that I didn't start seeing until later. That's also right about the time that "Chickenhead" became "CeeLo Green."

With all due respect to Kermit the Frog, I must say that for me it's actually been pretty easy being Green—and definitely much easier than being known as Chickenhead. At the time, I was always wearing the color green, and that went into my thought process. But also back then Sleepy Brown told me that I had a voice like Al Green—which is high praise indeed because the Reverend Al is clearly one of the all-time greats. In my mind, changing from Thomas DeCarlo Burton into CeeLo Green came to mean that I was a natural—it suggested that I was born to do this. I knew I would certainly be the one and only CeeLo Green. Like Ol' Dirty Bastard would say, "There's no father to my style." And in my life, there had been no father at all, just a void I kept trying to fill. So in choosing my own last name, in redefining myself as CeeLo Green, I think that was a way for me to say once and for all that I was my own man. And the Dungeon was the perfect place to invent myself as my own masterpiece.

I was already writing raps, making beat loops using a floor-model dual tape player, trying to figure out how to produce and arrange. But I knew I would need a lot of help and there was no shortage of talented help in the Dungeon. Out of nowhere, or so it seemed, Organized Noize and the Dungeon Family became like a Motown in Atlanta, creating a whole new Sound of Young America as Berry Gordy and his winning team had once done in the Motor City. Our sound was very genuine, very honest, very vulnerable, very moody. There was a lot of musicality, with live instrumentation. We seldom used samples. And the songs talked about a common knowledge that pertained to all parts of the country, all people.

In a flash, Organized Noize was in demand to make hits for everybody. (They would go on to write and produce some of the biggest hits in the whole world—we're talking global smashes like "Waterfalls" by TLC, on which I gladly and proudly sang background vocals, and "Can't Let Go (Love)" by En Vogue.) Meantime, the Dungeon Family was growing into one big tangle of talent and ambition, tied together by history and blood. Gipp even married Joi, a singer who was also part of the scene. So the Dungeon Family was real family. But in music and organized crime, being part of a family can really help or really hurt.

The main players in the Dungeon Family were young

guys from the Dirty South who had big egos and even bigger chips on our shoulders. As young men with fresh attitudes so commonly are, we were all in a rather big rush to stake our claims and make our marks. So the atmosphere in the beginning wasn't exactly "All for one and one for all!" For us, at first, it was more like "Let's all keep pushing like hell in the same general direction until one of us finally breaks on through to the other side." That way, we figured, once one of us made it through the front door of music's big time, then we would keep the door ajar long enough for all of us to flood into fortune and fame.

As fate would have it, the Dungeon Family's first breakthrough arrived in late 1992 when Organized Noize was able to place our little brothers OutKast's track called "Player's Ball" on the LaFace Christmas album called *A LaFace Family Christmas*. At the time, OutKast's playful Yuletide effort stood out in a very big way. Here was this really strong, really street rap track on an album full of much slicker seasonal soul and R&B material. Looking back now, this was the moment when our gang finally began to move out from the Dungeon and get our first peek at the outside world of possibilities. OutKast getting one of their songs released proved to us that the same thing could happen for all of us.

That was the good news. At the same time, having Out-Kast break out first from the Dungeon Family also led to a little confusion as well. As a result of the order of events back then, Goodie Mob became wrongly seen by some as just being part of OutKast's scene, and for the record, let me tell you why that's not quite right. If anything, the reality was actually more like the other way around. With Goodie Mob and OutKast, the love was mutual and that love was genuine too. But let me be perfectly clear here—it's definitely not like they just gave and we just took. If anything, we gave more than we got in terms of influence. See, André and Big Boi from OutKast and I are the same age, but in terms of experience, I felt like I was an Original Gangsta and that experience gave me the standing of an elder alongside them. For me and the rest of Goodie Mob, they were the younger generation.

Big Gipp: The relationship between us and André and Big Boi from OutKast was always competitive, but always friendly and always close too, because we were all part of the Dungeon Family. Sure, we could argue with one another, but make no mistake, we stood together against the world. In the beginning, OutKast learned a lot from us. We were the big brothers, they were the little brothers. In our minds, OutKast never overshadowed us because we weren't trying to do the same exact thing. We always tried to make sure there was a distinction. And at least the way we saw it, we were always equals.

The way I saw it, Dré was a quiet gangster who would not say much back then. Big Boi was very flamboyant, but there was also a slight awkwardness there because unlike all of us Atlanta boys, Antwan was from the outside world—specifically, he was from Savannah, Georgia, which may not sound like it was too far, but to us that was a whole other world. There were a lot of things that transpired as kids between CeeLo and the OutKast duo, so that by the time they met up again at the Dungeon, they all shared a lot of history. Meanwhile, me, the Organized Noize guys, and Khujo and T-Mo, all came from the other side of town.

And if you listen to the first OutKast album, you notice CeeLo and me were really solo artists then who were kind of Mob-adjacent. In the beginning, Khujo was in charge because he was a serious gangster back then. Khujo's name was even bigger and louder in the street than Lo's had been because of all the stuff he had done. So Khujo commanded a lot of respect. T-Mo also commanded a lot of respect, but in a different way because T-Mo was personally real quiet. T-Mo had been adopted as a child, and he was usually by himself and only messed with those he really had to mess with. T-Mo never had a lot of people around him, but he was a fighter when he had to be and a damn good one. We always said Khujo was the meat, T-Mo was the vegetables, CeeLo was the water—because what he has to say is crystal clear. I was the glue that somehow kept the whole meal together.

People looked at Goodie Mob like we were a little scary no matter what we did. People were intimidated by us, and maybe they had some reason to be. As a group, we stood for something, and we stood strong. If Goodie Mob had said something soft and safe with the music that we made, I don't think we'd be remembered today. But we wanted to say something, and at the same time, we might really kick your ass if you didn't listen to us and agree.

Remember, the Dungeon Family was like a collective—we were very deeply associated, yet all separate entities. Out-Kast and Goodie Mob had two totally different dynamics. We couldn't be the same unless we tried, and I give you my word, we didn't try. As proud as we were for our Dungeon brothers, we weren't an offshoot of them. We weren't broken, so we didn't need any fixing. And we were too crazy in our own right to ever want to borrow their brand of crazy. That said, OutKast was family to us and they did a lot to help spread the word about us.

Listen to that first album, *Southernplayalisticadillac-muzik*, and you'll hear Goodie Mob represented on two tracks—on "Call of Da Wild" and more famously on a very cool number called "Git Up, Git Out." Gipp and I co-wrote "Git Up, Git Out" with the OutKast guys and more than any other track, that's the one that helped me make my point of entry into the hip-hop pantheon. It also brought together all the elements of Goodie Mob for the first time.

"Git Up, Git Out" is a politically charged statement about the need to take charge of your own destiny and go out and do something in this world. It's an inspirational street message that struck a big chord with all of us because it expressed exactly where we were in our lives at that very moment. It was intensely personal, and universal at the same time.

The reaction to the track was strong and immediate: For the first—but not last—time people in the music industry started talking about me. As a result of doing the verse for "Git Up, Git Out," I was named Doper's Rhyme of the Month in *The Source* magazine, which was an extremely sought-after honor back in the day. What made this honor even more meaningful to me was the fact that "Git Up, Git Out" was my very first-ever recorded verse—my real entry into the game. Just on the basis of that track, I was actually offered a few different solo record deals.

I thought long and hard about whether I should strike out on my own as a solo artist or forge ahead as part of Goodie Mob. The more I debated the issue, the more I felt that it would have been a conflict of interest for me to fly solo at first because my new musical older brothers had been waiting in the wings. To me, taking a solo deal back then would have seemed out of order and inappropriate to the other guys in Goodie Mob and to Rico Wade from Organized Noize who was playing a huge role in terms of producing what we were doing. I thought that I should do like Spike Lee would want, and do the right thing. At the same time, I also figured maybe there would be some safety in numbers for me. We weren't strangers in the least bit, and I felt comfortable with each one of the guys. And in my heart, I felt like I wasn't ready then to make it as a solo artist—at least not yet.

So when it was time to make a deal, I signed on with the Mob.

Along with Organized Noize, the most important ingredient in creating the sound of the Dirty South was LaFace Records. Back in 1989 Antonio "L.A." Reid and Kenneth "Babyface" Edmonds opened up shop as a joint venture with Arista, hoping to hop on the emerging Atlanta music scene. L.A. and Babyface had started out in an R&B band called the Deele, and as far as we were concerned, they were the deal we all wanted to make. L.A. had signed our sisters in TLC and was helping them put out platinum albums. OutKast was their first foray into rap. Goodie Mob was next.

The first time I met L.A. Reid was at an OutKast picnic in a mansion they'd rented outside of Atlanta. Biggie Smalls was just coming up, and he had opened for Out-Kast, so they had a really nice party. I knew L.A. Reid from the Deele, so I just started talking to him. I've never been excitable around people like him, because I'm so well informed and familiar with them. If I have the opportunity to speak with them, I know how to impress. L.A. took a liking to me, almost immediately. Who knows why? People said we favored each other. I guess I could see that we had a lot in common, although we never spoke about it much. He was a drummer, and that's what I originally wanted to be before I realized I could program a drum machine. We're both Geminis. And, as it turns out, he likes women as much as I do! Since those days, L.A. has gone on to become one of the major power players in the music industry, now heading up Epic Records. But who would have guessed that years later we would be on rival music shows, with L.A. as a judge on the *X-Factor* and me on *The Voice*? As the Moody Blues would put it, "Isn't Life Strange?"

LaFace Records signed Goodie Mob in 1994. The way that I saw it, Goodie Mob was like an exciting new family of old friends. Fundamentally, Goodie Mob was some serious fun. For all of our differences as individuals, our shared love for rap—and a few bad habits—brought us together. We all loved the name Goodie Mob. It just had an impressive ring to it—we were not to be fucked with lightly. Later on a track called "Fighting," we explained that Goodie Mob stood for "The Good Die Young Mostly Over Bullshit"—which too often is still too true. Ultimately, we ended up giving the name Goodie Mob our own meaning with all of the music and all of the attitude we brought to the music. And as the record shows, Goodie Mob may have been short on big hits, but we were rarely if ever short on attitude.

Big Gipp: A lot of our friends didn't make it out of high school. We were just lucky because we found something else to do when other kids didn't have anything. Music saved all of us.

Other kids thought we were kind of weird to be into music; they thought you had to be from New York to rap. We were trying to buy turntables and mics while kids were buying drugs. Of course, came the time, we were also selling drugs. And we were the type of guys who ran to the fights, we didn't run away from them.

I used to sit in the trap house, where they sold cocaine. I'm a mellow guy and I didn't like the way the customers acted, because they would act so crazy. I was the dude sitting in the cocaine trap, but I was selling weed! CeeLo never really sold drugs, but he was always around us. Khujo and T-Mo, we were more into it than André and Big Boi and CeeLo 'cause we were older than them. So they used to watch us and follow us into those scenes, but after some of our friends started dying from it, it started getting so close to us that we just had to realize that what you put out in the world, you get back. Those the rules.

Bean was a friend who died on the basketball court. He's in a Goodie Mob song. Another one of our friends, Spanky, got killed right after he was in a video with us and OutKast. We did the video on Friday, had a show Saturday night, and came home to find out he was dead. Somebody had come into the house and tried to rob him and they killed him. It was like the first time we started recognizing that the things that you do in the dark will come back to haunt you.

We recorded our first album, *Soul Food*, at the home studio of the one of the greatest music men of all time, Curtis Mayfield—who was one of the leaders of the Impressions, for whom he wrote twentieth-century soul classics like "People Get Ready" and "We're a Winner." Then as a solo superstar, Curtis cut unforgettable soundtracks for *Super Fly* and another movie classic called *Sparkle*. Truth be told, I'm not even sure now why we recorded there. I heard stories that maybe our producers, Organized Noize, were discussing buying the home and the studio. In retrospect, if we were there, it was probably because we got a very reasonable rate. Knowing Goodie Mob and our situation then, a good price was probably more incentive than the sense of music history or any kind of nostalgia.

Curtis Mayfield—who was paralyzed in a stage accident in 1990 and passed in 1999—was not around the studio at the time we were recording. But his stuff was still in the house. There was a room filled with reels from *Super Fly*. Gipp even went into his closet to borrow a sweat suit that he wore on the jacket cover of *Soul Food*. So in a way the album is infused with his spirit. And I believe that Curtis Mayfield is still around anywhere people are making good, soulful, and socially conscious music. Which is exactly what Goodie Mob was trying to do.

Right from the start, Goodie Mob wasn't just trying to get a hit record. Fools and geniuses that we were, we dreamed of changing the world. We wanted to be like Public Enemy for the Dirty South. We wanted respect as much as we wanted hits, and as with Public Enemy, we felt as if it would take a nation of millions to hold us back. And even against a nation of millions, we liked our odds.

There had been Southern rap before us, but a lot of it wasn't very good or very deep. We wanted to bring Southern hip-hop newfound respect with albums that were intelligent and progressive, like the work Public Enemy had done on the East Coast. *Soul Food* was in essence a compilation of the things we had all been doing as individuals. Taken as a whole, it was pretty tough stuff, dark, political, angry. Gipp acted almost like our group's alderman—he's always had a strong political point of view. He was once a member of the Nation of Islam and was always enlightened in terms of politics and social consciousness and had a savvy for social media before people even called it that. I think Gipp brought a lot of that edge to the music that we made. Honestly, I'm not really like that so much—I'm all heart. So while Gipp brought the politics, I brought my own kind of soul and gospel aspect to the music of Goodie Mob.

Church roots run deep—even for sinners like me. No matter what I had done wrong by that time—or whatever I still might do someday—the fact is both of my parents were ministers. I always loved gospel music because it spoke to your soul. Music at its best is religious, it is spiritual. It is a practice. It is a faith. It's sincere. It's supernatural. It's extraordinary. It's surreal. It's a paranormal activity if you will. And in the wrong hands, sometimes it's a sin. My musical life began in church, and therefore in some ways it became about praise. And if you praise and exalt, it's an act of selflessness. I still think of myself as only being the messenger. Look at Goodie Mob's first album cover, and it looks like we're praying to do our job right. Take a listen to "Free" on *Soul Food*, and there's not much confusion about where I was coming from then.

"Free" was the song I wrote about my mom, and I wanted it to be the first song on our first album. Her journey was full of amazing grace and terrible pain. For all our difficulties, I loved her deeply for everything she had given me. And in her suffering, she was about to give me the most miraculous and supernatural gift of all.

CHAPTER FIVE

Getting Up and Getting Out

Endings and Beginnings

My Momma, destination unknown,
   went out on her own
She was barely even grown and
   became my Momma
I never knew my dad, so even when
   the times got bad
I was glad cause I had my Momma
For so long she had to be strong
I know at certain times she was wrong
But she still my Momma, it still amazes me
The Lord had to help her raise me judging
   from the way I used to be
My Momma, the biggest player that I know
   I love her so
Hell everything I got I owe to my Momma

—Goodie Mob, *"Guess Who"*

GOODIE GOODIE

I love sharing the stage with the guys in Goodie Mob,
now more than ever.

Photo by Catherine McGann/Getty Images

The longer that you live, the more that you discover that life is an epic journey—one that is made up of a seemingly endless series of beginnings and endings.

In most of your finer epics, feelings of overwhelming joy are closely tied to moments of devastating loss. The secret of life—revealed here for the first time anywhere—is realizing that all of it is part of life's rich tapestry. As someone far wiser than me once noted, we all have to begin somewhere. And as we all learn sooner or later, we all have to end up somewhere too. But life does not transpire on our schedules, and sometimes our beginnings and our endings seem to take place at the same times.

One door opens.

Another door shuts forever.

And so it came to pass that just as my mother began her long, slow, and painful fade in her earthly journey, the Goodie Mob and I started our rise to the top—or wherever else we would end up.

———

Something told me to go home. I had been living with a friend while we were in the studio making *Soul Food* when

I decided to move back in with my grandmother and my mother. I guess I knew my mom was nearing the end. She was sick all the time, and often in the hospital. The truth is that I'd hardly ever lived with my mother because of the insane and scattered lives we both had lived as we improvised our ways through this world. So I was not always tuned in to her state of mind. But my intuitiveness was very advanced, and something told me that I should move back home around that time. I believe that kind of foresight came in part from my street sensibility. When you're living the street life, you have to be able to feel when the heat is around the corner. I had a kind of criminally advanced skill set that was sharpened from experience. When you're living on the edge, you have to have that sixth sense.

I moved into the den and I tried to help to the best of my abilities. My grandmother was recovering from another hip surgery, and she was hobbling around, trying to nurse my mom. Shedonna was living with Aunt Audrey, coming over every night to give Grandma a break. But our grandmother was coming down with serious stomach problems too. The whole thing was wearing her down, and the situation was looking very grim.

I have never been a man who focuses much on regrets. Maybe that's because I have done too many things I could regret if I ever took time to focus on them. But I do have one regret from that time when my mother was dying. There was this one night I was at the house, feeling tired and irritable, and my mother had to be turned in her bed.

She sensed that I didn't want to help her at that moment. She looked at me and said, "Well, the Lord knows if I could do it myself, I would." I hate that memory. I hate that I reacted that way.

But even though she was dying, she was still my mother, and strong in spirit. She was concerned for my soul, and she was a formidable presence. Gipp told me he could feel it the first time he met her—which happened to be the day she learned that I had joined a group called Goodie Mob. We were making our EPK—electronic press kit—and filming at locations all over Atlanta. We had done some filming at my aunt Audrey's apartment complex— that's the one you'll see in the "Cell Therapy" video. And then we wanted to do a scene with my mother, where I rise up out of her body. It was kind of a surprise to everyone the afternoon I showed up at my grandmother's house trailed by a video crew and Goodie Mob.

"Momma," I said. "We're making our album for real." She just looked back and forth between the cameras and my crew, which I must say was a colorful bunch. She knew something was happening.

Shedonna tells me that this was the day when my family realized I was serious about making my life in the music business. But my mother was still very tied to the church and she didn't approve of secular music. So for our mother, having her only son grow up to become a rapper was a pretty big no-no. She didn't want to know about my music, right up until the time she passed away. Shedonna told me she begged her to listen to an advance CD of the first Goodie Mob album, but Mom would say, "No, that's of the devil! I'm not listening to it." Then one night, out of the blue, she told Shedonna to put on the CD and let her listen to it. I was on the road, but Shedonna called me from the back bedroom and said, "Guess what? Mom is listening to your entire CD."

"What? No!"

"Yeah, the whole thing," Shedonna said. "She hasn't turned it off yet!"

I think it was her way of just making sure that I was okay and that I had a positive message for the world. Shedonna believes that on some level she knew what was going to happen in my life, and she approved. She never said anything to either of us, but she didn't have to. She listened, and we knew.

Around this time we were doing all kinds of traveling to launch Goodie Mob, and I remember being on a plane sitting next to T-Mo and telling him, "I think I'm about to face the biggest test of my life. I think I'm going to lose my grandmother and my mother at the same time." I believe that my mother saw my grandmother getting weak and began the process of sacrificing herself. Deep down, I sense that my mother felt that no one ever could—or would—take care of her the way my grandmother did. So I'm sure she felt that if her mother wasn't going to be around, then she didn't want to be around either. The last thing my mother ever asked of me was for me and Shedonna to visit her together in the hospital. Usually, my sister would go, and I'd come by later, after she was gone.

But on that day, we rode down to the hospital together. As we were walking into her room, the doctor was walking out and saying "Okay, Sheila, if you don't eat, we're going to have to put the tube down you." My mother had this look on her face, and she said, "Don't you let them be putting any tube down me." And we were saying "Well, Mom, you've got to eat if you want to live. I guess if you don't want to live, you shouldn't eat." My mother said, "Don't you run any of that reverse psychology shit on me." We just had to laugh. At the time, I didn't realize what she was doing. Not then. Not at that moment.

Some days in your life fade away instantly. Other days are never-ending, and stay with you forever. I remember Goodie Mob had just gotten done doing an outdoor concert at Clark Atlanta University. This particular night really sticks out in everyone's mind. We were on a very high stage, and at one point in the show I drank from a water bottle, shook it up a little, then sprayed it on the crowd a little and threw the bottle out there in the crowd for fun. Someone in the crowd threw the bottle back hard, and it hit T-Mo right in the face. Now, that might not make me flinch these days. But back then, I was a young man, someone you should never push because I was always close to the edge. I had a total hair-trigger temper—real reactionary in that way.

So I just took off and dived into the crowd, and the audience parted like the Red Sea as I fell to Earth. My chest hit the ground and there was a large and loud *SPLAT!* like in a cartoon. I slid because it was raining and muddy that night—which may also explain why the crowd wasn't really in the mood to be sprayed with water. For my foolishness, I ended up cracking my shoulder—and it's still cracked. By the time I somehow got back up on my feet, Khujo had jumped off the stage and was miraculously standing right there beside me trying to help. I still don't know how Khujo got to me that quickly. That's why I love him still. We may have fought each other in Goodie Mob sometimes, but we also fought for each other when the need arose—like that night, when the need fell hard.

I was able to put my arms around Khujo, and he had to walk me off because I had knocked the air out of myself. I guess I had a lot of hot air, even then. After the show, I went to a friend's house and had a few beers for the pain. Then I went home to my grandmother's place and crashed in the den.

On so many occasions in my life, when the phone has rung late at night, it's been because someone has passed or some other terrible news. I'm a light sleeper, and as a result, when that phone rings late, I always jump. I think that anxiety also comes from having to feel like the protector from a young age because even then—by the process of elimination—I was the man of the house, or as close as we had. Growing up, every night I'd walk around the house in my paranoia and check the windows and the door because there wasn't a dad around to do it—and sometimes not a mom either.

The call came that night and my grandmother rushed to tell me "Okay, Lo, let's get up and go to the hospital.

They say Sheila is on life support." I remember me not necessarily knowing exactly what that meant, so my grandmother said my mother had already stopped breathing on her own. Ten minutes later, just as we were getting ready to leave, they called again from the hospital and said that she had passed. And I just remember my grandmother crying "Why did you all let her die like that?" And I don't know why she said that—maybe it was just the first words she could get out of her mouth.

I was the only man there, and I couldn't express any hurt at the moment. I had to wake my sister up and deliver the terrible news. It was so hurtful. We all had such deep, sad, but mixed feelings. You have to understand, by this time, my mother had been suffering so much and was so argumentative with everybody that it was a kind of relief when she finally passed. I think that was her way of trying to make sure we all missed her a little less—which was exactly the sort of thing she would do.

I had to try to be strong. We all drove out to Shepherd Spinal Center in Atlanta where she had been staying. They told us a pulmonary embolism had finally killed her. I stood for a while by her hospital bed and touched her hand. She was so cold. The life source had left her body. I felt compelled to fall into prayer, and we all stood around her body and prayed.

With her death, I couldn't deny her anymore. She became a part of me in a very profound and spiritual way. I truly believe my mother bestowed me with her life's work and with her strength and her drive. It was like passing the torch. In the end, that's my true inheritance, and to me, it's priceless.

At least in my head, I decided her suffering was not in vain. On some level I cannot fully explain, I began to feel that she sacrificed her life for me, as if there were some strange transfer of her energy and spirit and wishes from her to me. And in my heart of hearts, I truly believe that my mother knew that she somehow saved my soul with her life. At least, that's how I feel about it. So everything that I have ever done, she's done too. Because my mother is always in my head and in my heart, I've written quite a few songs for her, including "She Knows" on the second Gnarls Barkley album with the lyrics, "Gonna be just like you, I'm giving my life, too."

Some moments are private, but here's what can I say: I spoke at my mother's wake and I sang gospel at her funeral. I just stood up unannounced and unscheduled, and did it completely by the spirit because no matter what, I am my parents' child. Thinking back, I can't believe I did that or got through it. But like I said, with all the pain, there was joy too. At last my mother was free.

Big Gipp: The passing of CeeLo's mother graduated him to being a man. He recognized that there are consequences to the things that we do in life. Overnight, he had to take things more seriously, and he did. When we got word that his mom had passed, I remember looking at Lo and he didn't cry. He was so strong that it was almost like his mom was there with him, giving him support. As far as dealing with death, I had the sense that CeeLo was at peace with it at the time. He was at peace with knowing that she didn't have to hurt anymore. And he didn't have to worry about her suffering anymore. So in a way, her being free of suffering freed *him* up to grow up, take charge, and work like a beast to make it.

CeeLo had started out relatively happy to be along for the Goodie Mob ride, but almost instantly, it became clear that he's a man who wants to do the driving whenever he can. Remember, Goodie Mob had started as Khujo's group, but CeeLo always had big and crazy ideas and would not be shy about expressing them. He was pushing us to go farther out—and places beyond anything rap groups did. I remember CeeLo saying things like "Okay, Gipp, we're all going to wear jumpsuits with gas masks!" CeeLo loved the wildness of rock and roll fashion. Then and now, CeeLo is—first and foremost—a true artist who loves to push boundaries and buttons whenever he possibly can.

When we first started going into the studio to put Goodie Mob songs down, Organized Noize would put a song up and one of us would just listen to it and jump on it. Not CeeLo. He would listen to it, and then he'd rearrange it and tell us all what to do. He was always the one to ask the question, and then he was also the one to give the answer. I never got involved in that, but CeeLo always took it upon himself to make whatever he was doing better. He put songs in a kind of storybook lineup so that they added up to say something, to tell a story, to make the music a journey. That's what he does, and he does it better than anyone else I've ever seen. And he did it with soul and style. It was like he was arranging a meal, and it all had to work together and it all had to taste good. He was busy making something out of nothing, and I think that's the story of CeeLo's life. The story of his life is taking something that nobody may even see the beauty of, seeing what it can really do, and being the one who's always able to take it and shine it up and make it seem like a brand-new toy.

Goodie Mob went out on our first tour opening up for the Roots and the Fugees, and that's when my relationship with Lauryn Hill began. I felt a powerful connection with her immediately. We're both Geminis, the same age. Lauryn's birthday was the same as Dré's, and mine was two days later. She's very nurturing, comes across like family. So we were just like brother and sister, although I confess that I once thought she could have been my soul mate. She saw something in me that I may not have recognized for myself. This was right before I met my future wife, Christine, and for a moment, I thought Lauryn was going to be my queen, the love of my life. True confession: I loved Lauryn Hill. I wanted to marry her, and I thought she was made just for me. That didn't happen, but we still got to have a great friendship that ended up making a big difference in my life.

When we signed with LaFace Records, they gave us a check for $20,000—$5,000 each. Even after our first album was out, Goodie Mob's financial reality didn't change that much. But I was cool with that, I didn't even want massive success all that much. The truth is that being famous was never my dream. I wanted something constructive to do with my life, have a real purpose in the world. I was more preoccupied with being an activist than with being some kind of superstar.

So I talked. A lot. Touring for our first album, I would do fifteen minutes of dialogue onstage. I was preaching, basically because to me it really was the family business. I was also trying my best to explain the music. I didn't think the *Soul Food* album was all that enjoyable, honestly. I thought it was listenable and high quality, but it sure wasn't one of those "put your hands in the air like you don't care" party albums. At this time we were deadly serious about the music because we were soldiering, trying to solidify the South as someplace worthy of respect in hip-hop. So we went out on the front lines to make sure that we were respected—that we were counted. That's all it was about for me in those days. We had a mission and a purpose. Right there, right then, we wanted to forever abolish the stereotypes about Southern rap—that it was less meaningful and political and relevant than the music coming from New York or Los Angeles.

I think it's pretty shameful that some of the Southern artists who followed us have reinstated certain old stereotypes. But back then we were four Southern guys with a mission, and we were carrying a whole lot on our backs, and in a way it weighed us down at the time.

L.A. Reid from LaFace Records thought we were taking ourselves too seriously. One time when we were back from the road he had us over to his house. "You're young guys!" he said. "Why so serious all the time? Ain't you getting no pussy?"

Our second Goodie Mob album called *Still Standing* was an easier process for me. The four of us rented a cabin in the Georgia woods and mapped out the concepts. Then I got my tonsils taken out and I was in bed for two weeks. It gave me some time at home and time to actually sit with my notebooks and write my rhymes and think my thoughts. There wasn't a lot of freestyling or small talk for me. For me it was about a lot of big ideas—and just the facts, ma'am. Personally, I liked our second album even more than the first. I still love the song "They Don't Dance No Mo' " and the crazy video we made of it which featured me as a dancing baby with moves like Michael Jackson. The wild sense of humor that I display now, I was displaying back at times then too, but people didn't really know me yet so they didn't always get the joke at all. Around my friends and family, I've always been a pretty funny guy, but definitely back in the Goodie Mob days, the perception around us was so serious because we were pushing some deadly serious ideas. But on my own, I have always loved making people laugh. I found that it felt a lot better than making people scared—which is something I also knew all about.

There were some dark themes in that second album too, because it was a dark time. Tupac and Biggie Smalls had both been killed, and the East Coast–West Coast beefs were ripping the Hip-Hop Nation apart. We'd known both Biggie and Tupac, so it was personal. In fact, we had just been out on the West Coast, talking about doing some recording with 'Pac.

Big Gipp: Our path in Goodie Mob was not like anyone else's. You could see our ending in our beginning. And you could see our beginning in our end. On one level, we had the perfect start—our first album, *Soul Food*, went gold and had three songs that made the Top 10 on the rap charts—"Cell Therapy" went to number 1 on the rap singles, then "Soul Food" went to number 7, and finally "Dirty South" went to number 8, with all three songs making the Billboard Hot 100 Pop chart too. Our first tour was amazing too and became iconic because it featured us along with two other great groups who were coming on strong then: the Fugees and the Roots. That's a whole lot of talent right there, and everybody got along great. We were all one big, happy, freaky hip-hop family all out to take over the world with music and soul.

It meant even more to us because we didn't sell out with some dance party, we came out of the box saying something that was tough and no-nonsense. We were not just fighting to make our name, we were fighting for the prominence and the respect of Southern hip-hop. And we were winning. In Goodie Mob, we did not view ourselves as some "act." We viewed ourselves as musical messengers with a word to spread. And we were proud of being monthly guests on a BET show called *Teen Summit* then and doing our small part to educate black kids about their history a little. But the first time I totally realized that CeeLo has a gift way beyond just music was when we met with Minister Louis Farrakhan. Now that was a day to remember, when CeeLo ended up doing some ministering of his own.

Around this time Minister Farrakhan from the Nation of Islam called together the rap community for a big conference in Chicago to create some kind of coalition, a sort of peace treaty to try to unify the hip-hop world and stop the war that was brewing and likely would have continued. That day we were going around the table and everyone was discussing this, that, and the other thing. And when the microphone came in front of me, I preached. That's the only way that I can put it. And if you've ever been to a black church, you know what I mean. Maybe it was genetic, considering my heritage. In any case, something kicked in and I found myself opening my big mouth and giving my own hip-hop sermon about the need to stop the madness and start spreading a better world. I was inspired that day. I started talking about what was going on and about what we needed to do about it, and I could see all these faces listening intently, and the older men in the room in their suits were looking impressed, like "Young man, wow."

I so wanted to be part of a moment and a movement that was positive and had meaning. Like a lot of reformed criminals, I might have made an excellent priest, as long as there was no vow of celibacy. That day I wanted to join the Nation of Islam and just be a soldier in a struggle that was worth fighting for. I guess this may sound a little morbid, but I always dreamed of an honorable death more than I wanted infamy. I wanted—and want—my life to mean something. It's *got* to mean something.

I remember thinking perhaps this was the purpose on Earth my mother and so many others at church had spoken about. Over the years, people who met me on the street would tell me, "You have the mark of a minister on you. You are going to preach someday." Even people from other churches would tell my mother that. And in a way, it made sense. After all, I'd always worn suits, tried to carry myself like an older man, even carrying my father's pipe. Maybe I was supposed to take my rightful place as a preacher and a soldier for God. It was a temptation— and a good one in my mind—but it wasn't quite my path, as much as I genuinely respect it. After that day, I realized that I would have to preach a different gospel in the end—my own Crazy Gospel According to CeeLo Green. But before I would find my own funky flock and write my own Good Book, I would have to journey in the wilderness for a little bit longer.

CHAPTER SIX

A Self-Civilized Man Meets His Match and Our Mob Breaks Apart

This is out of respect to women period
I'm quite single
And occasionally I mingle
But aside from all the rest
She sparks my interest
No ma'm I don't know you,
Just offerin' the common respect I feel
    I owe you...

You're my beginnin', my end
You're my sista lover and friend
God is your light from within
It shines through your beautiful skin.

    —*Goodie Mob, "Beautiful Skin"*

FAMILY MAN

Here I am with my beautiful wife, Christine, the daughters
we raised together, Kalah and Sierra, and our son, Kingston.
I will always thank God for my beautiful family.

The song "Beautiful Skin" was more than my salute to the pleasures of the flesh—female flesh, that is. It's a love letter to women everywhere. That was a song I did one day in the studio when no one from the Mob was around. I had the idea and a friend of ours named Chris Jewell had a track, and the melody to that song came when we were beat boxing. Initially, that song was almost like a Bobby McFerrin kind thing—my strange take on "Don't Worry, Be Happy." We playing around in the studio doing something like that, and I remember that's where the melody came from. Lyrically, "Beautiful Skin" became my salute to sisters everywhere. The fact is that even before I met my match, I've just always appreciated women, all women, and especially our women. But woman in general are so beautiful to me. They most certainly are a wonderland, enchanting and very interesting. To me a woman is a muse and amusing. You can get understanding from a woman, but I don't know if you could completely understand a woman. They are mysterious, and who doesn't love a little mystery in their life? Or a whole lot of mystery if you can get away with it? Hell, I am a man of mystery. That's still the case with me, from then to "The Lady Killer" and beyond.

I loved Christine Johnson from the very first moment that I met her. I remember spotting Christine at a birthday party for Gipp around the time of *Still Standing.* She was a vision of womanhood, towering above the competition. She had a singular kind of mutant beauty—in my mind at least, she was the much more gorgeous Queen to my highly unusual but still rather regal King. Christine is taller than me, and back then she looked even taller because she wore her beautiful hair in stacks, with these amazing blond dreadlocks—something that none of us had ever seen on any sister before. As a result, she appeared to be approximately nine feet tall of something good indeed. Like they say, big things sometimes come in tall packages. So I suppose you could say that I have always looked up to Christine—both literally and figuratively. Then there was the fact that Christine had a gorgeous face and beautiful skin. And as soon as she began to talk, I knew right away that I had met my match. As even a kid should know, when you play with matches, sparks will fly.

After the party, I got in a two-seater Benz with Sleepy Brown, from our Dungeon brothers Organized Noize. Christine just jumped in the car with me and we rolled back to the Dungeon, which had by then moved into an urban mansion with white columns. I do not think I really knew the complete meaning of the words "love" and "lust" until that moment. Okay, there were probably a lot of words that I didn't know the meaning of back then, but you get the idea. I fell instantly for this woman—and I fell hard.

So it was love at first sight for me, and for her—well, it was pretty instant as well. See, you might be surprised, but I can be a fairly charming fellow when I really need to be. At that time, I really needed and wanted Christine. She was so strikingly beautiful and staggeringly different in terms of dress and style, she also reminded me to always be myself—a lesson I might have learned a little too well. The woman had so much style. She wore a lot of thrift store stuff—shabby chic they call it now—and she was tremendously well put together. Christine changed my life forever. She was as close to a soul mate as I may ever have here on Earth.

I love that old Neil Young song "A Man Needs a Maid." Some people find that sentiment sexist, so let's just all agree sometimes a man needs a mate and a family too. Christine already had two wonderful little girls, Sierra and Kalah, and so I had an instant family. I like to think of myself as a mostly self-civilized man, but Christine and the girls helped too. They taught me a lot about how to love and how to take care of other people—lessons that I learned later than most. Despite being a bit of a mutant all of my life, like most of your garden-variety human beings, I still love love, especially whenever it is reciprocated. I crave affection. I crave company. I crave family. I crave the stable home I never really had. Trust me, the things that you are denied early in your life become even more attractive to you later on.

During those first few years as the man of the house with Christine and her beautiful girls, I found a kind of strength inside of myself that I didn't even know I had in me. A few years earlier, I was a monster that people called "Chickenhead." Now I was a father figure to two little girls who called me "Dad." Being in any group is a lot like being in any gang, and for most people caught up in them, gangs are usually a kind of substitute family for those seeking some measure of safety in numbers. Now I had the real family I had always been looking for.

Big Gipp: CeeLo has always had a touch with women, and part of the secret is that he's not afraid of any woman. He doesn't care what a woman looks like. If she's close enough to touch, she's close enough to speak with him. If I had to sum up his attitude with women, I'd put it like this: I might not be her type, but if she gives me a little while to talk, I might just convince her. He's told me, some people have the look, and some people have to talk. That may be the secret to his impeccable wordplay—he needed it to get some play! I've seen women who thought they weren't his type end up all in his bed. He has the kind of vocabulary that gets women to use a very important word: Yes.

And right from the moment they met, CeeLo and Christine were completely inseparable. Those two were an amazing vision together. Of course, CeeLo has always stood out in any room that he's in, and I'm pretty sure that Christine was the only blond dreadlocked girl in all of Atlanta then. Seeing her for the first time was almost like spotting a rare, exotic, sexy animal living right in the heart of the Dirty South. Christine was way ahead of her time, and you could tell that CeeLo was instantly impressed with her style and individuality. Christine stood out as being totally unique, so she was probably the perfect woman for a man who may very well be a mutant. Once we mutants understand who we really are, the ridicule of the world doesn't matter to us because we are very strong in who are. Christine is a very strong woman. She filled a big void in CeeLo's life for love and for comfort and for family, especially since she had two young daughters. Christine was very adamant about raising her two girls right, and CeeLo admired this young, beautiful single mom who stood up for herself and for her girls. Think about it: Christine was really CeeLo's first serious girlfriend and eventually she became his first—and very possibly only—wife. Overnight he went from being a kid to becoming like a father to her two kids. Respect is big for CeeLo, and he respected Christine as much as he loved her—which was a whole hell of a lot.

At the same time, with Goodie Mob beginning to take off, I found myself increasingly wanting to be my own man. Yet as I would find out, being your own man and being part of a Mob—even our crazy and slightly unruly Mob—don't always go together. There's another song title on the *Still Standing* album that in retrospect defines me pretty well and at the same time suggests why there was trouble brewing between me and Goodie Mob. The song is called "I Refuse Limitation," and artistically that's always been my problem and my blessing. I've always been highly inquisitive, and that has kept me pushing while others might settle and stay and just let it be. So I did what I do, and I kept being myself, and pushed to show my own voice in the group, which I know rubbed some people the wrong way.

Still, we pushed on. Our second album went gold—and we even did a little cameo in a movie called *Mystery Men* with Ben Stiller, William H. Macy, Paul Reubens, and Hank Azaria as a bunch of lesser superheroes doing a song called "Not So Goodie Mob." The movie didn't do all that well, so I guess we remained a group of lesser superheroes ourselves.

Since Gipp had gotten married to the singer Joi and then I got together with Christine and her daughters, the road had become a tougher and tougher place. Suddenly, you're not just getting away, you're going away and there are people back home who miss you. Looking back, we went so quickly from being kids to having kids, and Gipp and I weren't quite so carefree after that. I loved the refuge from the world that Christine, the girls, and I could create together—so much so that there were many times when I just wanted to stay at home rather than be the kind of road warriors Goodie Mob had become.

My experience with Christine changed just about everything in my life. I now see that the situation became a little like Yoko Ono and John Lennon. John Lennon seemed to upset the balance of the Beatles by bringing Yoko into what that great group did, and being with Christine somehow made me suddenly and dramatically less interested in doing much of anything with the group.

After a while, being with Christine and her girls became my priority, at the same exact time that I found being part of a group like Goodie Mob just wasn't feeding me anymore.

This wasn't Christine's fault—or the fault of Gipp, Khujo, or T-Mo either. In retrospect, maybe it was all my fault. In any case, for my own reasons based on my own strange life story, I found myself beginning to want to be a part of a real family and beginning to lose interest in being one of the guys in any Mob and compromising any visions I might have—musical or otherwise.

Big Gipp: In Goodie Mob, we never signed a big publishing deal. We never became the biggest stars in the world. For the most part, we made our name and our money on the road—which is a dangerous place. We weren't out to sell the most records of anybody. We were out to save the world. I remember one time on the road we went past this church bus that had caught on fire. This was in the middle of nowhere while we were driving through Arkansas on tour. Well, we pulled our bus over and we started helping the kids. Finally, there was one more kid left on the bus, and our dude Tim Elkort ran up on the burning bus and got the kid and pulled him out to safety. And as soon as we got the kid ten or twelve feet from the bus, the bus exploded. It was amazing that no one got hurt. We got an award from the church. So we didn't get our Grammy, we got that instead.

The third Goodie Mob album, *World Party,* is when it all fell apart between the Mob and me. Trust me, making that album was no party. Our musical differences began playing out, and we fought about which way to go. From my perspective, having not made all that much money in the game to that point, the group desperately wanted to sell more records, and that just wasn't what was driving me at that time. We were less into making big statements than looking for hits. We brought other people into the process too. One track called "Rebuilding" was one of the first tracks ever produced by some kid from Chicago named Kanye West. In retrospect, it's very cool that we worked together, even if we didn't even meet at the time. There were a lot of meetings I skipped back then. I felt like we were regressing, turning our spaceship around and falling back to Earth. More and more, I was a man looking for the exit.

By then my old friend Lauryn Hill had already reached out to me and asked me to collaborate with her on "Do You Like the Way," a song that ended up being featured on one of the biggest albums of all time—*Supernatural* by Santana. I felt empowered by the project—artistically and monetarily. It was the first time I could really sing out on a vocal, and it affected me, gave me ideas of how things could be. Santana wasn't there the day we recorded, but I met him later, when we were performing the song for a TV show. He told me I had the voice of a thousand generations. I didn't know what he meant, but it sounded wonderful, especially coming from him. *Supernatural* won Album of the Year at the Grammys in 1999, and it sold 30 million copies. I figured it would put some serious change in my pocket.

Meanwhile, when the going gets tough, sometimes the tough get going in the other direction. I wanted a family. I wanted to be home. I wanted a life. And more than anything, musically speaking, I wanted to make my own statement without having to run it by or get approved by any committee—even one made up of my longtime Goodie buddies. So not for the last time in my career and in my life, I withdrew further and further into my own deal—both literally and figuratively. And once I discovered our management was ripping me off—and taking food out of the mouth of my new family—Goodie Mob felt like a much less welcoming, and even dangerous place for me to be. Gipp was there when I found out that I wasn't seeing all the money I thought I should be getting from the Santana album and I pulled a gun on one of our managers. I'll let him tell that story.

Big Gipp: My take on why CeeLo left Goodie Mob is a little different. For me, it was a low point that came from a high point for CeeLo. Lauryn Hill had reached out and worked with CeeLo on that track "Do You Like the Way" for Santana's *Supernatural* album, and it became part of one of the biggest albums of all time. After that, CeeLo had a dispute over a publishing check with one of our managers just as we were going out on tour for *World Party*. I remember Lo calling me and saying "Dude has some money from me, and I'm getting it back!"

The big showdown was between the manager and CeeLo, and we couldn't do anything about the money or the feelings behind the money because there were only two people in that fight. When our manager got on the bus that morning, CeeLo pulled some kind of Uzi on him. It looked like CeeLo was about to kill the man. And I stood in front of CeeLo and said, "You don't have to do this. You don't have to kill him for the money." And Lo said, "If I die, at least I'll have my respect." That's when I knew CeeLo was capable of pulling a murder when it comes to him fighting for his respect—or him feeling like he had been disrespected. CeeLo is a truly great guy—right until he feels like he's been treated with no respect, then trust me, he can be one *bad* enemy.

When the shit hits the fan with you and your best friends, it is the shittiest feeling of all. The day after CeeLo pulled a gun on our manager on the bus, Goodie Mob was supposed to start a House of Blues tour with the Black Eyed Peas. So I left with the group to go set up for the tour. Our first night was in Hilton Head, and I tried to speak with CeeLo all day that day trying to see if he was going to get on the bus or would he not get on the bus. That was the question. And soon the answer was clear—he wasn't going anywhere. That was when I finally realized there was going to be big division in the group, that CeeLo was going to leave Goodie Mob, and a very dark period in my life was about to begin. And it was worse because there was nothing any of us could do to prevent the situation.

The gun incident was probably a final nail in a coffin that was already being built. I withdrew from the tour and went on hiatus. I just took a year off and I didn't do much of anything. I don't think I left the house.

Meanwhile, OutKast was exploding, and where we had always been all over each other's albums and videos, now there were all these OutKast videos that I wasn't in, like "B.O.B. (Bombs Over Bagdad)" and later "Roses." I only sang on one song apiece on *Stankonia* and *Speakerboxxx/The Love Below*. I just pulled away from being a part of so many things then. After a while, I didn't feel like I belonged. I would much rather bow out gracefully than be argumentatively indifferent. Or maybe I wanted my conspicuous absence to be noticed and to be welcomed back warmly. Part of me wanted to hear the Goodie Mob guys say, "Come back, CeeLo, we love you, we miss you." But that was not the reaction I got. What I got was that people respected my space. So I took it, and more and more distance developed between us. That old Mob of ours was breaking apart.

Why does anything in this life fall apart? Generally, it's not for one reason but for many reasons. I had grown up in Goodie Mob, and I felt like I just grew out of it eventually. It's the most natural thing in a way. It wasn't personal. I was following my voice and seeing where that voice might take me. And that was the right thing to do because I can see now that a song like "Crazy" or "Fuck You" would never have happened under the banner of Goodie Mob. Those songs wouldn't have fit. And at least for me, art is not about being restricted. It's about being free to express. I am a restless artist and a restless man. I have a lot of songs in me to sing. All kinds of songs too. If I had not aspired to become an individual artist and not decided to take a chance and be the whole thing instead of just part of something, I would never have known what exactly was spinning inside of me. That would have been an injustice to all of us, and most especially to me. And time after time in my life, I have found that I am a man who truly hates injustice—especially when that injustice is happening to me. So not for the last time, I did what men do sometimes.

I left.

THE MATRIARCH:
My grandmother Ruby
Callaway Robinson. She
saw it all, and I'm so
thankful she was always
there for me.

THE MOTHER OF ALL MOTHERS:
My mother, Sheila Jeanette
Callaway, had a lot of strength in
her, and, sadly, she would need
every bit of it.

OH BROTHER, OH SISTER:
My sister and I grew up
together—okay at least she
grew up.

PHOTO OPPORTUNITIES:
Looking back, it seems like
every time Shedonna and
I were together, someone
was snapping a photo. And
there were no smartphones
back then, kids!

BIRTHDAY BOY:
Here I am with my
sister, Shedonna,
on my third
birthday.

SMILING FACES SOMETIMES:
Yes, there was a lot of pain in our
childhood, but there was
also a lot of love.

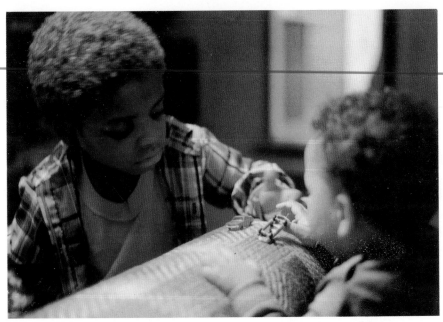

DRIVING AMBITION: As you can see in this photo of me as a kid, I have always loved fast cars.

KING FOR A DAY: Even back in kindergarten, I felt like royalty—and even then I could really rock a white suit.

RAP IT UP: Here I am doing one of my early Bible raps in elementary school.

A FAMILY THAT ROCKS TOGETHER: Shedonna and I aren't kids anymore. Well, maybe I'm still more of a kid than she is.

ALL MOBBED UP: The Goodie Mob looking pretty badass, if I do say so myself.

PROM NIGHT: Dress is formal, but the look of my face is unimpressed. This was my sister Shedonna's prom night.

GOODIE TIMES: The Goodie Mob, fighting for the good name of the Dirty South.

GOODIE TIMES: The Mob with our boys André 3000 and Big Boi of OutKast.

GOODIE TIMES: Here we are making our name.

GOODIE TIMES: And here we are becoming dads.

WHITE WEDDING: On my first—and as far as I'm concerned, only—wedding day to Christine Johnson.

GRANDMA'S HAND: My grandmother has always been there for me, like here in 2007 at a party for a little label I started called Radiculture. *Photo by Moses Robinson/WireImage*

TWO OF A PAIR: Kingston is two here. There's no one I love to see smile more.

FAMILY AFFAIR: Making the scene at the Primary Wave Pre-Grammy Party with the family in 2011. *Photo by Jonathan Leibson/WireImage*

Q & LO: What an honor to get to know the legendary Quincy Jones. This was at Elton John's Oscar party. And yes, I checked my ego at the door. *Photo by Michael Kovac/WireImage*

THREE'S GOOD COMPANY: I've been blessed to meet so many of my heroes. Here I am with Sir Elton John and Smokey Robinson—who's royalty in my book—at Elton's Oscar party in 2011. *Photo by Stefanie Keenan/WireImage*

A CHRISTMAS GIFT TO REMEMBER: What a honor it was for this former delinquent to share the stage with the First Family and so many more notables at "Christmas in Washington" in 2011. *Photo by Theo Wargo/WireImage for Turner*

I'M NOT LIKE A VIRGIN: But I was thrilled to appear with the one and only Madonna at the Super Bowl XLVI Halftime Show. The New York Giants won that day—and so did I. *Photo by David Bergman /Sports Illustrated/Getty Images*

A SHINING MOMENT: I take a nice photo. The car and the girl help too. *Photo by Meeno*

ME AND MR. STEWART: What an honor to sing with a rock god like Rod Stewart.

TREELO GREEN: I was thrilled to get together with my Muppets posse to help light things up at the 80th Annual Rockefeller Center Christmas Tree Lighting Ceremony. *Photo by Gary Gershoff/ Getty Images*

RIDING A WAVE: Gipp and I hanging with Larry and our Primary Wave team before the Grammys in 2013. *Photo by Garry "Prophecy" Sun for SunOfHollywood.com*

SCENES OF A SHOWMAN: It was a blast mounting *Loberace* for audiences in Las Vegas. *Photo by Alexander Stein*

SCENES OF A SHOWMAN: In my *Loberace* wig.

IF I CAN MAKE IT THERE: My eDiets billboard in the middle of Times Square. © NASDAQ OMX 2013, Rohini Shahriar

SCENES OF A SHOWMAN: A rehearsal for *Loberace*.

CHAPTER SEVEN

Perfect Imperfections

A Soul Machine Goes So Lo

Listen now, I got a story to tell
About a bird who wanted to fly away
You see he knew that he could and
    he probably would
But his family said they needed him
    to stay
But his spirit is strong and he's been waiting
    so long
And he don't really want nobody to tell him
    daddy wrong
So excuse me I wanna go and kiss the sky
Cause these wings that I was given were
    intended to fly

—CeeLo Green, "El Dorado Sunrise
    (Super Chicken)"

HARD TIMES

Doing what it took to make ends meet.

C eeLo was chosen."

That's what Rico Wade from Organized Noize once said about me, and who am I to argue?

Call it a strange sixth sense or arrogant delusions of grandeur about myself, but in my own funky heart of hearts, I have always felt that my story has been fated. Perhaps I feel this way because my life has been, in so many ways, stranger than fiction. Some of this stuff you couldn't make up—at least *I* couldn't. Maybe everybody out there shares this same deep feeling of the role of destiny in their lives, but since I have only ever had the pleasure of being my own mutant self, I will speak strictly for myself here. Yet even though I feel my path has been preordained, I still do not believe in just passively accepting your fate. Instead, I believe strongly in fighting for it. As the noted gangster rapper Donald Trump once declared, "What separates the winners from the losers is how a person reacts to each new twist of fate."

———————

Looking back, I believe it was probably inevitable that I eventually spread my wings from Goodie Mob and flew away to find my own musical destination. Yes, I may be a bit of a player at heart, but my record reflects pretty clearly the fact that I am not always in the mood to be a team player. For better or for worse—and usually for both—I was born to be my own man. Love me. Hate me. Hit me. Stroke me. But you sure as hell better not ever try to confine or define me.

Leaving is never that easy, and making the big transition from being part of Goodie Mob to becoming solo artist—a man in my own right—got downright tense and pretty ugly. By this time, things were changing in the Atlanta music world, and Goodie Mob had been transferred from LaFace Records in our hometown to the larger Arista musical mother ship based in New York. L.A. Reid—who was now leaving the Dirty South and taking over the big label—decided to sign me as a solo artist on Arista. Eventually, the rest of Goodie Mob left the label and signed with another independent company, Koch Records. Our split was complete and less than friendly. And like the old song says, breaking up is hard to do, and our breakup was no exception.

As the split of Goodie Mob became real, I took my sweet time making my first solo album. Christine and I also took a long time to get around to making our marriage official. But in 2000, we finally walked down the aisle at my grandmother's church in Cascade Heights. I remember that we later read an article about our big day and the reporter said that our wedding was "quaint and frugal." I thought shit, I don't even know what "frugal" is. I didn't know that people assumed our net worth was all that great then because trust me, it was not. People think all the musical artists they have heard of are rich and famous, but back then and especially now, they could be very wrong. L.A. Reid didn't pay for the wedding, but he sweetly paid for our wedding reception. Larry Mestel, the brilliant manager I have now, always jokes, "Remember, that reception was recoupable!" So I probably paid for that party one way or another because that is business as usual in the music business. But to me, it was a lovely gift and like the old Bill Withers song says, "A Lovely Day," filled with people we loved.

Of course my grandmother and sister and all the family was there, and a lot of Christine's family and friends came down from North Carolina to be with us. Because of the tensions still raging between us at the time, Gipp and the guys from my Goodie Mob weren't there. But we had friends including one of my all-time favorites in hip-hop history—the great Luke Skywalker of 2 Live Crew fame. That's right, folks, Luther R. Campbell, or as everyone in the world of rap calls him, "Uncle Luke," was at our reception. How do you like those family values?

Speaking of family values, Christine and I had always talked about having a child together, and right around the time of the wedding, we learned she was pregnant with a son.

That amazing news led me to do something I'd been meaning to do for a long time: I legally changed my name from Thomas DeCarlo Burton to Thomas DeCarlo Callaway. I wanted my son to have my mother's maiden name, because of everything I owed to her.

Big Gipp: I heard that CeeLo and Christine's wedding was great, but I wasn't there. That was during the troublesome time. But I heard CeeLo was happy, and deep down that's all I wanted for him.

It was a very confusing time for me and Khujo and T-Mo. Not only did we love the guy—we also needed him. We were a group that had turned down publishing deals and lived off the money that we made on the road. So when we suddenly couldn't live off the road, we all took a big hit. Without CeeLo, we were worth less in every way. We took a huge hit in terms of our livelihood, and creatively speaking, we took a huge hit when it came to how we were going to work and put out albums. It was a big mess figuring out how to work without a key player in our group like CeeLo. Whether we would have admitted it or not right at that moment, deep down we knew it was never going to be the same without him. Look at the guy; he is literally one of a kind. How the hell do you replace a man who's one of a kind? The answer is this: You can't, and you're damned if you even try.

It was a triple whammy on us, because the group had just lost CeeLo and our manager, and then we lost our record company. CeeLo and I both got calls from L.A. Reid to come to New York, saying "I'm going to give both of you your own solo deals." But that was at the exact brief time when CeeLo and I were not talking. With us now not communicating, still being on the same label would have felt like some sort of competition thing between him and me. My instant instinct was to opt out of that. At that point, I was so mentally disturbed by the situation in Goodie Mob, disturbed by my marriage to Joi falling apart, and disturbed by everything going on in our world that I just wanted out. I wanted out from the system we were in and the whole mess that was breaking our world apart. So I left Arista and went to Koch Records to do Goodie Mob records with T-Mo and Khujo. CeeLo stayed with L.A. Reid at Arista, and suddenly the brotherhood between us seemed like it was gone forever.

In retrospect, if we had all stayed on the same label, we would have been pitted against each other and there would have been even more bad blood. But for the record, L.A. Reid was always great to us—from the day he pulled up at the Dungeon to shoot OutKast's first video for *Southernplayalisticadillacmuzik* with Puff Daddy by his side, L.A. Reid was always the innovator, but he always listened to Goodie Mob about what we wanted to do and he put his best dollar on us being able to do that. How can you complain? So it's amazing to look at what he's become, and all the superstars he helped build even after he left LaFace. It's just a testament to how great of a record man he is, and that maybe he's the last of the great record men who is still kicking it and making music history.

We decided on a home birth for Kingston. I was still on my extended hiatus from the road to be a husband and the head of a household. I wanted to make sure I was in place to witness the birth of my son and not somewhere else that was less significant to me. Looking back, I was so happy to be there every step of the way. Coming from where I had come from, I knew about dads who were not there—and I wanted to be there for sure. I got into the birth process just like I got into any other creative process. I truly studied the logistics.

The baby was born in the bathtub, what they call a "water birth," and it was a truly awesome. During the whole birth process, I just tried to be very supportive of Christine, walking her up and down steps, giving her a routine so that she wouldn't sit there idle and in pain. I was there beside her for the whole miracle. It wasn't scary for me, but then again, I don't scare easy. Watching our beautiful son come into the world was profound, and I was content and confident and certain about who I was and what we were doing. Maybe for the first time in my life, I was completely proud of what we had accomplished and what we aspired to do. My sister, Shedonna, was around for Kingston's birth, and she was pregnant herself at the time. When Kingston finally made his entrance, we all joined together to pray for this precious boy.

Right from the very first second I saw Kingston's face, I saw my mother in him and thankfully I saw lots of his gorgeous mother in him too. I'll tell you something real, when I first saw him, I thought about that saying "Your daddy's rich and your mama's good lookin'." Well, okay, maybe I wasn't exactly rich yet, but I was kind of famous, and I still felt like maybe on my way. And thankfully, Kingston's mother was beautiful in more ways that one—and she still is too. The truth is that I prayed that my son would favor my wife and not me, and that prayer was heard. He was and is perfect.

In my mind, Kingston was a beautiful thought and idea that gradually became a very beautiful kid. And I knew deep down that my son would be better than me—because he has my best intentions at the core of me without all my flaws, physical and otherwise. I am a king who some see as a freak. We called him Kingston because he is royalty, and looks like it too. To me, Kingston's arrival proved that my intentions are righteous. Those intentions go way beyond what I had to do and had to be on occasion along the way. I vowed that he would have a different life than I'd had. In my mind at least, I have had to slay dragons so that he won't have to. I will never be a perfect man, but to me our son, Kingston, already is.

How did I learn to be a good parent? Father is written in me; it's the way that I am. Others doubt you for long enough, you begin to doubt yourself. But now I saw that

I had it somewhere deep inside me to become the father I never had. Absence makes the heart grow fonder, no more than that.

I was definitely a diaper-changing kind of dad. I was a home dad. We were living out in Fayetteville, Georgia, and life was good. I love being at home like that. Even to this day, if I could hit the lottery for a hundred million, I wouldn't be out and about doing half the shit I do.

In the weeks leading up to Kingston's birth, I had played a lot of music around him and spoke to Christine's stomach and prayed over her stomach too. Maybe that's why my son was very quiet as a baby. He didn't cry one bit. He's still pretty quiet like that. But my sister remembers how worried I was that Kingston had inherited some of my less desirable traits.

"Of course, as mischievous as Lo was as a child, there was that deep fear for him that his son was going to act just as bad as he was," says Shedonna. "And back when he was very little, Kingston would come up and hug you very close and sweetly—because he was sweet then and he's sweet now. But then after he hugged you, and before he completed his embrace, he'd sometimes bite you just as hard as he had just hugged you. And let me tell you, that scared the heck out of Lo. He flipped out, like 'My son is going around biting people—he's going to be trouble just like I was!' Kingston grew out of it, but Lo was *so* worried he would be a terror. My grandmother and I had to laugh, and we knew somewhere up there, my mother was laughing too."

As in all truly epic tales, there comes a time when the hero undergoes some terrible trials. Just when it looks like he's about to reach his goal, he suffers a supreme ordeal. Like Luke Skywalker finding out who his father is, Han Solo getting frozen in carbonite, or even Jonah ending up in the belly of the whale, every hero has to be dragged into darkness before he can emerge in triumph. Your very own supernatural hero was no different. Just when I thought I had it made—a growing family, a new record deal, a solo career about to take off—the ever-clever Creator threw some serious roadblocks my way. And this otherwise uplifting story of redemption took some sad and ugly turns.

The way I saw it, producing and recording my very first solo album was my big chance to create something on my terms and strictly my own terms only. I have always been first and foremost a totally instinctive artist, not a trained one, and those creative instincts were telling me that I had to try to get somewhere new—somewhere that wasn't anyplace I could imagine going with Goodie Mob. And as usually happens to me when I come to a fork in the road, I felt the need to take a strong left turn and find some new virgin territory for me to deflower.

In other words, it was time to start dreaming a new dream. That's the funny thing about being a part of a group. In the beginning, the dream is simply to become a great group. But once that first shared dream comes true, people begin to dream their own dreams, and mine was not one that I felt like sharing. I knew that my next path would have to be my own—however bumpy that road might get. And it helped that I had L.A. Reid, one of the top players in the music business, in my corner and backing me in my first heavyweight title fight. I think L.A. bet big on me because that was a time when my buddies OutKast broke through with their *Stankonia* album, and a whole cool neo-soul world seemed to be all over the airwaves. The possibilities seemed endless. In any case, it sure felt like there were great expectations riding on my broad shoulders.

With my mentor large and in charge, Arista gave me the artistic freedom to go out and produce an entire album that I heard in my head. I got the kind of liberty and the license that Prince got early in his career. That's big, and it doesn't happen anymore, as the music industry has declined and changed and become obsessed only with the bottom line. The fact that a weirdass album like *Cee-Lo Green and His Perfect Imperfections* even exists at all represents L.A.'s investment in me and his very real support of me.

One reason why the album is called *Perfect Imperfections* is because beyond the fact that I am clearly a perfectly imperfect character, I knew that I was taking a big creative leap with the album. I took that leap willingly, knowingly, and quite happily. At the time, I didn't realize how crazy it was to produce myself and make the album with such an unrestrained and some might say irresponsible sense of freedom. For me, it felt right and normal to me to use the recording studio as my playground because that's what greats like Brian Wilson, Sly Stone, and Prince had done before me.

There's no doubt that *Perfect Imperfections* was one crazy album to make, but in my mind, it was a good kind of crazy. It may not be the best album I ever made, but it sure was a fascinating and dangerous place to start. Listening back to it today, I still love the album for its ambition, for its range, and for its utter insanity over the course of 73 minutes and 16 seconds of my distinctive musical craziness. To me, *Perfect Imperfections* sounds like the debut solo album from a very interesting guy. Okay, to be honest, it actually sounds like the debut album from a whole bunch of interesting guys with multiple personalities.

Please don't hate me because I contain multitudes of talents. Even by my standards, *Perfect Imperfections* was a very eclectic piece of work where I got the chance to invite everyone I loved to my party—from Big Gipp to John Popper from Blues Traveler. To show you where my head was at then, the opening track, "Bad Mutha," featured a sample from "Wounded Knee" from Primus' *Pork Soda* album. I loved Primus because they were freaks like me.

That said, I could only imagine what was going through L.A. Reid's head when I took a good deal of money from Arista and then handed him this thoroughly crazyass album. I'm pretty sure that when he first heard *Cee-Lo Green and His Perfect Imperfections*, it was an album that inspired awe, but not necessarily the good kind of awe he might have been hoping for—more like shock and awe. To me it felt like the reaction was "What the fuck is this, and how do I sell it to anybody? I know this guy is someone special, but who the hell would that someone be?" But being such a supportive figure in my life, L.A. Reid supported my first album as much as he could.

I thought back about this just the other night because I went to do a bit with Will Smith at the Kids' Choice Awards and my old friend L.A. Reid—who is now chairman and chief executive officer of Epic Records and recently a judge himself on *X Factor*—brought all his kids back to hang out with me. I wasn't expecting any company backstage that night, so it was very cool to catch up with my old friend and booster. To me, L.A. turning up meant that either his kids are fans of mine and it was their request—or L.A. was showing me off to his children because, in a way, I'm one of his kids too. Thank you, L.A., always for being an early believer and a friend.

The record was finished and there was no going back. And on April 21, 2002, my time had come, and I finally released my first ever-solo album. If I do say so myself, that album made a whole lot of noise. Unfortunately, almost no one who wasn't in the studio actually ever heard all that noise because almost no one bought it.

To be sure, there were some rave reviews for *Perfect Imperfections*. In *Vibe*, for example, a clearly very astute

critic named David Bray wrote, "The son of Baptist ministers, Cee-Lo has always had a lot to say. His vocal skills
are matched by lyrical language rooted in the preacher
tradition—as eloquent as it is wise. He has long sought
spiritual truths with an honest acknowledgement of his
human shortcoming (see album title) and he tackles
weighty, real-world subjects with a sense of perception
that is rare among writers in any field."

Unfortunately, not many people got to hear all that
truth I was sharing on *Perfect Imperfections*. Not for the last
time, the rest of the world thought that I was all over the
musical map and that no matter when they stopped on
that map, they still didn't hear a big hit single. Of course,
the truth is that as an artist, I am still all over the place,
but in much smarter ways now. I do all sorts of things all
the time, but now my wide-ranging talent strikes people
as being genuine. It certainly doesn't hurt that I'm world
famous now. Still, it all comes down to being true to be
yourself. I'm not trying to be anyone else.

Looking back, I probably wasn't tough enough on
myself as a producer. For instance, I wasn't even concerned with radio singles. I stopped listening to the radio
long ago. I listen to great music wherever I can find it, and
whenever I can make it, but I never dial it in. Those of us
from the Dungeon Family didn't come from the point of
view that it's all about getting the right single. We didn't
make radio singles. We just made the coolest shit we could
come up with—and for me there were all sorts of cool shit
on *Perfect Imperfections*. I am still proud of so many songs

on the album, like the very wild and wonderful track "El Dorado Sunrise (Super Chicken)"—one of my grand statements about moving on from the Mob—and very personal "Gettin' Grown" that was like a little musical memoir in its own right.

Still, without any breakout radio hits, I had to try to get hands on about promoting an album like *Perfect Imperfections*. Some people said that I was going to hate performing alone without a group, but I have never been shy. For me being a solo artist wasn't that lonely. I was having fun, showing the world what I could do—and revealing more about myself, and I'm not just talking about the tattoos I'd show the crowd. Even as a solo artist, I still had a bunch of people up there onstage with me. In fact, around that time, I began to gather a few of disciples around me—my first entourage. That will happen in this business, especially until the money runs out.

There was one song on *Perfect Imperfections* that I felt could have broken the whole thing wide open for me. That song was called—what else—"Closet Freak." I knew that track was strong. That groove was strong, and the concept was clear. And the word "freak" just always seemed to fit me because let's be imperfectly clear here: I am a freak. I will stand up and own being a freak every chance I get. I have been called every kind of freak you could ever imagine, and I love it. But in the end "Closet Freak" was not the big breakout hit I hoped it would be. Still, I knew that track worked when we went to Columbia, South Carolina, for an appearance we did in a strip club there. Boy, "Closet Freak" was an absolute smash in that room. All the wonderfully nasty ladies onstage were dancing to that song, and they took me from the stage and started dancing on me. The night got a little hazy at the end, but I remember all the girls in the club got in a line and gave me little lap dances. We had a real romp that night. So at least in Columbia, South Carolina, one crazy night, "Closet Freak" was one of the biggest and most meaningful "hits" I ever had. That's the kind of success story I really respond to.

In retrospect, I probably didn't help the song's chances one bit when we made a crazy video to go with it. Coming on the heels of Goodie Mob—which was so stern and serious and almost militant and military—"Closet Freak" basically begged people to think I was gay before that was quite so widely accepted. That could have been career suicide, but I did not care about such things. Basically, when I put on a wedding dress and called myself a "Closet Freak," I was letting my freak flag fly in my own freaky way, even though some people took that song as me coming out of the closet. I was doing no such thing—trust me, if you ever see me coming out of a closet, there will be at least one pretty lady with me. For me, "Closet Freak" was just a great funk number, and I love funk—now, then, and always.

Who survives that besides CeeLo Green? Yet I knew I had to keep jumping because as it's turned out, some of my biggest successes have been my biggest leaps. Look at what I have always done with my life—I basically jump off an edge and learn how to fly. I don't want to be a false idol or try to sell people some compromised idea. I'm not here to wallow in a cesspool and squeeze out a few dollars. I am here to fight hard and try to say something.

———

As much as I hated being away from home, I tried to stay out on the road as long as I could to support *Perfect Imperfections*. But I happened to be back in Atlanta that June when I got another one of those bad phone calls that I always dread. This time it was Khujo's wife, saying there had been an accident.

I rushed to the hospital as soon as I heard, and suddenly there we all were in the waiting room. It took a near tragedy to bring Goodie Mob together again. At least for one day.

It turned out that Khujo had been at the Dungeon until about four in the morning, and he fell asleep at the wheel driving home. When he woke up, his car was going through a guardrail on the side of the road. As the car rolled, that same guardrail went all the way through his car and pinned Khujo's leg against the floor. The emergency workers had to cut him out of the car and save him, thinking it might explode. So he had to watch them cut his leg off below the knee.

He was still in surgery when I got to the hospital, and it was a terrible scene, with the women crying and everybody so worried. Seems like the whole Dungeon Family was there. We forgot our differences for the moment, remembered how we were brothers. But then we went our ways again. Thank God Khujo pulled through, but he was a long time healing. And it took a lot longer still to heal the hard feelings between us.

Goodie Mob was a touring group, and now Khujo needed a lot of rehab before they could get back on the road. It was a hard time for them, to say the least. But by then I was already starting to think about my second solo album, and I had no intention to get back together at the time. I had marked my own course.

Gipp, Kujo, and T-Mo eventually went into the studio for their new label and came out with an album called *One Monkey Don't Stop the Show*. The media had a lot of fun suggesting that I was the departing monkey in this situation. People said some of their songs were about me and that some of mine were about them. Those people may have even been correct some of the time. But what people did not know is that however much we might have argued, and fought and cursed each other, there was always a connection. Even when we weren't seeing each other much, there were secret lines of communication. Gipp and I always spoke, even though the rap media was writing about how we were at war. I had invited him to appear on my first solo album. There was no doubt that we would always be in each other's lives, some way or another.

While all this was happening, things were getting rocky on the home front too.

Like a lot of marriages, ours had its ups and downs. And as far as I'm concerned, I don't owe anyone an answer to shit that's happened in my personal life. That is why it's called a personal life. But I will take this opportunity to set the record straight on one incident that keeps popping up in the media. Because our lives are so publicized these days, you sometimes have to speak on behalf of your life and even defend it. This isn't my defense case but my honest attempt to clarify the misunderstanding that some inquiring minds like to spread.

This particular incident dates all the way back to July 2001. Christine and I and were not getting along at the time and had separated briefly, but we were still trying to keep things together. We had driven down to Disney World in Orlando, Florida, on a family vacation, and had enjoyed an entire weekend together. Then, on the way home, I was dropping off Christine and the kids, including Kingston in his baby seat, because I was staying somewhere else during our separation. As lovers do, we had gotten into some dumb dispute, and after we unpacked the car and the kids had gone inside, I felt as if Christine was being really dismissive of me. I hate feeling dismissed, especially when I felt like I was trying my best to do a good thing by attempting to keep us together as a family under difficult circumstances.

There I was standing in the garage with the door slammed on my face. I thought "Oh shit," and I felt years of anger and frustration and pain coming back to me. I felt hurt, and so I wanted to hurt something. I felt terribly slighted, and as I stood in the garage, some of my old street rage returned to me. At least in my crazy mind, there wasn't much I could really do—other than take out all of my frustrations on the first thing that I saw. So I grabbed the thing nearest to me—a little wooden statue that I found in the garage—and I busted the windows out of the Jaguar.

Yes, I know this was horrible behavior—something I have had some experience with over the years. But for the record, what happened that day really was vandalism and not domestic abuse like some people think. No one was harmed in this incident—other than that statue and that car. Christine didn't even know it happened at first—that garage was soundproofed, and she must have come down later that night, because she called me up and said, "Why did you do that?"

"Because I was frustrated," I said.

"CeeLo, that's the only means of transportation we've got," she said. "You know you have to pay for it." I said I was sorry and apologized because it was crazy. And it was.

In the end, I sure did pay for it. What happened was when Christine filled out the insurance form she, disclosed the nature of the incident. Two days later the police got involved and threw my ass in jail. I was arrested and released on $2,800 bail. For the record, I was not charged with domestic violence. The experience was humiliating, even though the mug shot wasn't too bad. A couple months later, I was taken back into custody after I failed to show up at a court arraignment. I've never been too great about showing up on time. In the end, I pleaded guilty to a single charge of "disorderly conduct"—which I have been guilty of most of my life—and spent two days in jail and a year on probation.

I fucked up. That's pretty clear. But just for the record, worse things have happened when two people argue. Sadly, worse things happen all the time—and people end up dead on both sides of domestic disputes. That is not what happened here. Thankfully, this was something stupid, not something tragic. It did not end the relationship between Christine and me. It didn't even end our marriage.

But as you might expect, my personal life had become suddenly a little bit messier following that Jaguar incident. I did spend more time rebuilding my relationship with Christine and the kids, and trying to keep the peace between us and earn their trust again. The time had come for me to behave myself and get right back to work. So in the wake of that passing storm, I figured I would try my best to stay out of trouble and focus on trying to get my music right.

We tried to make it work. But eventually in 2004, Christine filed for divorce. The truth is that even our divorce didn't end our relationship—it just changed it. Even though we're not together, my ex-wife and I, we're still a family, and a pretty functional one. And we still love each other like a day hasn't gone by. As much as anything else in this life, love is crazy—and I'm not the first one to see that or the last. I may be crazy, but I won't let anyone tell me I don't love my only wife or that she doesn't love me. And nothing or nobody will ever tell me that this union that led to our beautiful Kingston was any kind of mistake or failure.

A guy who I used to work with once called me an "idiot savant." At the time, I thought he was calling me an idiot, so I didn't act too thrilled. Now I think I know what he was trying to say. When it came to music, I didn't apply any math to the process whatsoever. My approach to music was and is entirely chemical. I did what came naturally to me and to my own idiosyncratic chemistry. I am like a human lava lamp. So in retrospect, maybe he had a point. When I'm making music I try to be totally innocent—not totally naïve, but innocent; not ignorant, just innocent. I think that attitude separates me from a lot of other artists today because so many people sit down at this particular table and the first thing they ever say is "Whose throat do I have to cut? What do I have to do to make it at any cost to anyone else?" I didn't want anything from anybody. I just wanted to make music. I didn't make *Perfect Imperfections* to hog up a budget. I made it because I was by myself following my muse—and that's just what came out then.

For the follow-up to *Perfect Imperfections*, I tried my best to play a little more ball and bring in some other producers, but still the fact remains that the late great Sammy Davis Jr. was right—I've gotta be me. I mean, in the end, who the hell else can I be?

Still, I tried to be open to more input and collaboration. On my next album for Arista, *Cee-Lo Green...Is the*

Soul Machine, I worked with some of the hottest names in music, like Timbaland and the Neptunes, as well as Jazze Pha, DJ Premiere, and my old pals Organized Noize. I still didn't—and couldn't—keep my freaky side in the closet, but I think we made a slightly less eccentric, somewhat more commercial album, especially tracks like "The Art of Noise," "I'll Be Around," and "My Kind of People."

But my timing was bad because shortly before my album came out, L.A. Reid moved on from Arista to run his next empire, the Island Def Jam Music Group, and suddenly there was a whole lot less interest at Arista in being in the CeeLo business. There were small glimmers of success—like getting to perform "I'll Be Around" with Timbaland on the second season of *Chappelle's Show,* but whatever we did, it wasn't enough to get a hit.

Big Gipp: CeeLo was so much more than hip-hop. CeeLo was—and is—way too big a talent to be contained by any group or any genre for too long. He always wanted to do it all—and so when he became a solo artist, that's exactly what he did. The great thing about CeeLo is that he is a true force of nature. Of course, the bad thing about CeeLo also is that he's a force of nature. No man or woman or group or record company is ever going to control this man for too long. As I've learned time and time again, the best way to get CeeLo to do anything is to try and tell him he can't do it.

CeeLo once told me that when he did his first solo show for Arista, he walked up onstage with a boa and a wig. He knew that he was scaring people, but that's one thing real artists do. They are scarily talented and they take chances. It's about freedom. CeeLo loves his freedom, personally and creatively. I know that for his second album, CeeLo tried to work with the right people—including big name producers like Timbaland and the Neptunes. CeeLo tried to do what other people do. But what works for everyone else just doesn't work for CeeLo. The man plays by his own rules, and he breaks those too. He didn't want to only write songs about the club, because CeeLo's world is bigger than that. And so is his talent.

Maybe CeeLo's first two solo albums didn't work because he dove into singing with two feet. Remember, he had been known first and foremost as a rapper before that. Everything CeeLo ever wanted to do and try, he did it all at once on those two solo albums. He tried to do every genre of music, and what he found out is that the music industry's attention span is just not that wide. People like an album of R&B songs, of love songs, but not an album that's like Noah's Ark with some of everything. CeeLo did it because it was something he wanted to do. He felt like those two albums were his boot camp for becoming a solo artist after pouring himself into being part of a group. Once he got out there on his own, he realized it was going to be a lot of work to establish the brand of CeeLo Green, Solo Artist. That took him a long time, and he's still in the process. The masters like Stevie Wonder or Michael Jackson figure out who they are musically then take everyone along for the ride. CeeLo is still defining himself as an artist— which is cool because there are still many mountains for him to climb.

In the end, Arista didn't drop me exactly—they just sort of released me because my contract was basically up. The company thought *Soul Machine* was a lost cause and didn't want to put any more money behind it. They gave me the choice whether I wanted to start something new or be free and just move on. As I always tend to do, I choose freedom because I thought they were all wrong about *Soul Machine*. True to form, I believed that I was right and they needed to see the light.

But first there was darkness. When I left Arista with no particular place to go, I found myself entering a kind of musical wilderness. Suddenly I was looking for my next meal or record deal. Between the *Soul Machine* album failing in 2004 and Gnarls Barkley coming out of nowhere in 2006, money got tight, but not too tight to mention here. I did not know where my next twenty grand was coming from. At the same time, I remember feeling a certain welcome sense of freedom and liberty. That's one nice thing about finding yourself in the wilderness—other than debt collectors, people don't bother you too much. And coming from where I had come from, being counted out and underestimated just made me feel very much at home.

CHAPTER EIGHT

A "Crazy" Great Odd Couple and Our Gnarly Trip to the Top

My heroes had the heart
To lose their lives out on a limb
And all I remember
Is thinking, I want to be like them

—*Gnarls Barkley, "Crazy"*

THE CRAZY FORCE WAS WITH US
Danger Mouse and I gave an out-of-this-world Gnarls Barkley performance of "Crazy" at the 2006 MTV Movie Awards. No, I am not Danger Mouse's father, and he turned me to the Dark Side.
Photo by John Shearer/WireImage

They say it is always darkest before the dawn—unless, of course, dawn never actually comes.

In a strange and now-distant land called 2004, the unusually dashing hero in our increasingly twisted fable of fame and misfortune found himself feeling more than a little bit lost in the wilderness. Okay, make that a lot lost. And right around this time in my story, I was getting increasingly tired of having my big black ass kicked hard and often by a truly scary monster called Life. By this point, I had already been called a promising artist many times, but for whatever reasons, it looked like those promises weren't being kept.

To recap some of the preceding bad and the ugly— because there was not a whole lot of good coming my way at this particular time—I was by now pretty much broke. Like the old song from the eighties said, there was basically nothing going on but the rent. I was single again, and I was now trying to pay alimony and child support without getting a whole lot of support myself from anywhere. To make matters even worse, I found myself drifting back toward complete obscurity after leaving Goodie Mob to go solo—and instead heading nowhere fast.

Yet even though record companies didn't believe in

me then, or possibly even remember me, and my phone wasn't exactly ringing off the hook, I have always believed in myself deep down—even when there was no reasonable basis on which to do so. You have to believe that you've got something to offer this world in order to survive in such an insane and unknowable business. After all, I have been a long shot all of my life.

Still, when the arc of your career begins to resemble a funky free fall, you do begin to wonder a little—is my story already over? And if not, where is my next happy ending coming from, and what do I do with myself in the meantime? Here's the answer I learned the hard way: If life gives you lemons, then you damn sure better find a different delicious flavor of lemonade to sell.

For a time there in the early twenty-first century, I got to a point where I didn't even want to be a performing artist. So I started to write and record with another talented artist named Tori Alamaze who was from our scene in Atlanta and sang backup on songs for OutKast. Tori became my muse for a while and, to my surprise, I really enjoyed taking a giant step behind the scenes. After brutally banging my head against a few studio walls trying to transform myself into a big solo artist, I must say that I found it very pleasurable to sit back and just write and produce. As I would find out again years later on *The Voice*, when I'm not smiling for the camera, I really enjoy the process of helping others take their rightful time in the spotlight—especially when I'm getting paid well for my time. In a funny way, trying to make Tori into the star she deserves to be was a welcome change of pace for me. I liked that it wasn't about me being a star but simply about making music, which is what I always wanted to do in the first place. And that, as best I can figure, is how I came to help write and produce a song that you might have heard of called "Don't Cha."

Ladies and gentlemen of the juke box jury, there are some songs that forever define their times, powerful protest statement that speak to the underlying political truths of our society. "Don't Cha" was definitely not one of those songs. But it was one catchy joint about the wonderful ways that women can tempt men and totally screw with, at the very least, our heads. In my mind, this instantly infectious and fittingly funky ditty was the song that would make Tori Alamaze into a household name. And for a while there, it really looked like our plan was going to come to fruition.

"Don't Cha" became Tori's first single for Universal, and for a hot minute there it looked like the record was going to be a big hit for her. But it got as high number 53 on the Billboard R&B Singles chart—and then just stopped. Dead. So close—yet so far away. Sadly, before long, the record label dropped Tori. But thankfully for me, you can't keep a great song down forever. So just a little while later, the very same song, with a few new sexy touches, became a major chart smash for the Pussycat Dolls. I produced "Don't Cha" as the group's very first single with a strong lead vocal by the top Doll Nicole Scherzinger and the great Busta Rhymes rapping on the track—probably because no one would have cared much then about me rapping on it at that point, and I always loved Busta's attitude. Finally,

I had my big hit—even though many people didn't and still don't realize that "Don't Cha" came from my dirty mind. The song went to number 2 on the Billboard Hot 100 and number 1 on the Hot Dance Music/Club Play chart. It became a truly sexy global sensation in 2005, reaching number 1 in England, Ireland, Australia, New Zealand, Belgium, Germany, Norway, and Switzerland, where I'm sure gorgeous little Swiss misses are still singing along to it in some chocolate shop. This was my first taste of international success—and I loved it.

The Pussycat Dolls doing "Don't Cha" didn't exactly make me a star, but it sure as hell helped make me solvent again. This surprising brush with the big time meant that my family and I were able to eat a little better, and trust me, it was great news when I really needed some. At the time, I remember saying to myself, maybe I've finally got myself something here. Maybe I will just write and produce the rest of my life and forget about all the frustrating craziness and maddening mystery of being an artist myself. But just like other lovable crime figures before me, every time that I think that I'm done, something or someone drags me right back in.

Suddenly out of nowhere—well, almost out of nowhere—my life went "Crazy" in the best possible way, and that craziness took me to some unexpected places.

The true story of Gnarls Barkley is the unlikely tale of two complete weirdos who somehow completed one another—

at least for a little while. I am proud to say that I am one of those weirdos, and the other is the international man of mystery who would be Danger Mouse.

I first met Brian Joseph Burton—who named himself Danger Mouse after his favorite British cartoon series—back when I was with Goodie Mob. At the time, Brian was living in Athens, Georgia, studying telecommunications. He and some friends competed in a talent contest and won the chance to open up for OutKast and our Mob at a gig we did at the University of Georgia.

For better or worse, love me or loathe me, I do tend to make a big impression on people one way or another, and something about my winning personality must have made a big impression on Danger Mouse. But Danger Mouse later told me that something I had said in an interview he read really spoke to him. He explained that he was strongly attracted to the idea of working with me because he read that I loved Portishead, a very cool British trip-hop group that he just happened to love too. He thought any black man who says he likes Portishead had to be his kind of guy. He had a point too—because Portishead was everything that I wanted my music to be too— dark, moody, hip-hop, and cool on its own terms. Their sound was eerie and inventive and beautiful—all things that I look for and treasure in music and in life too.

Backstage after the University of Georgia show, Danger Mouse handed me this instrumental demo tape to check out. Something about the darkness in the music spoke to me because, let's be real—as you have already noticed, a lot of my life has been dark. But it was the last we really saw of each other until around 2004 or 2005, when I laid down some vocals on *Danger Doom*, a freaky album Brian was producing with MF Doom. That was when we picked up the conversation where it had left off, and in a serious way.

By any standard, Danger Mouse and I were a truly odd musical couple—with me in the role of a much less pale Oscar Madison to Danger Mouse's Felix Unger. Thank God the two of us never tried to share an apartment. Personally speaking, we were really night and day, or at least dusk and dawn. For instance, Brian is quite slight and, as you may have noticed, I'm a slightly larger target. Back in the day, Brian was so shy that he dressed up in a mouse outfit so that he could meekly hide in plain sight. Lord knows I have been accused of many things in my life, some of those charges coming from the authorities, but being shy has never been one of them. But for all of our differences, Danger Mouse and I connected through music and found, at least temporarily, some very fertile common ground to toil on together.

By the time we started to created the gorgeous global monster that became Gnarls Barkley, Danger Mouse had begun to make his own oddly cool name thanks in large part to *The Grey Album*, an amazing and utterly unauthorized piece of work that combined the vocals from *The Black Album* by Jay-Z with the musical performances from

The White Album by the Beatles. Originally put together for the art of it and the shits and giggles of friends, *The Grey Album* soon became one of our world's first great viral hits. Like all things viral now, the music spread like wildfire over the Internet and eventually became one of the most talked about and argued over albums of the twenty-first century. The illegally impressive and wildly cool *Grey Album* made Danger Mouse a global star, a digital outlaw, and a world-class troublemaker—all clearly very good things in my book—namely, this book.

So how did people react in the secret hidden chambers of the music industry when Danger Mouse and I started to work together? The answer is: I don't know, because we didn't give one damn about what people said. We signed with an independent label, Downtown Records, that was run out of someone's Manhattan apartment. Like LaFace, Downtown was a joint venture with a big label, in this case Atlantic, so we had a lot of backup firepower if we took off. And then we did precisely what great artists have always done so well—we just got busy creating our own shared reality and then tried that crazy quilt we made together on for size. There was no other way of knowing if this unlikely partnership would work. After all, we were not two of a kind but a couple of crazy mutants who met in the dark and created a spark of something bigger than both of us.

In retrospect, I can see clearly why we didn't call our new musical partnership CeeLo Green and Danger Mouse—or Danger Mouse and CeeLo Green, for that matter. Which one of our names would have come first anyway? Trust me, that subject alone is something we could have argued over for hours if we had wanted to. Instead, we just got down to what was most important— the music—and the name came second. From what I've heard, while Brian was tossing around names with some of his friends, he almost called the group Bob Gnarley, but he liked the sound of Gnarls Barkley better. For my money, Gnarls Barkley is as absurd as any other memorable rock and roll name, from the Goo Goo Dolls to Oingo Bongo to Kajagoogoo. Yes, our name sounded weird, but it's also immediately unforgettable. With all due respect to Charles Barkley, I didn't immediately like our name when Danger Mouse first mentioned it. Honestly, I immediately hated it. Okay, for the record, I still don't like it. But however goofy it may be, the name Gnarls Barkley is pure quirk, and I have found that quirk works—at least it works for me. Although for a long time after our albums came out, people walked up and called me Mr. Barkley. A lot of them still didn't get that we were a group.

Now with a little distance and time I can say that Gnarls Barkley—the beautiful mutant musical love child of Danger Mouse and myself—is one of the great left-field success stories of all time. My solo career taught me the hard way that try as you might, you simply cannot be all things to all people. Too often, if you try, you end up being nothing to nobody. Before Gnarls Barkley brought my voice to the world, I was going nowhere as a solo artist because I had tried so hard to go absolutely everywhere.

Somehow working with Danger Mouse gave me a kind of focus that I needed to show the world what I could do.

I've described Danger Mouse as the picket fence around my wildflowers, and for me at least that just about says it all. Danger Mouse is many things to many people, but somehow when we worked together, his process kept me inside some boundaries and, in the end, that framing made me look even better than I do on my own. Working with Danger Mouse was the first time someone took me and actually tried to truly produce me. And in retrospect, that made Brian look like a genius because either he was very, very strong or no one bothered to notice that I could be very submissive too. Truthfully, I think that it was a balance of the two because it isn't like Brian is all that aggressive a dude, and I sure as hell ain't soft. I may not be a criminal anymore, but I still won't let anyone else ever steal my treasured sense of self.

Something in Danger Mouse's music did resemble the wonderfully odd eternal rhythm that exists somewhere inside of me, so in a way it was easy to write words for him. To my ears, the music that the world has come to know as Gnarls Barkley sounded like the score of my soul—the wild combination of words and music and texture and sound captured a kind of controlled chaos.

But like a lot of odd couples, Danger Mouse and I also have a way of rubbing each other the wrong way. I can only guess what he would say about me, but I would describe Danger Mouse as neurotic and narcissistic. He's clean and neat, but also very meat and potatoes. In fact, all I that have ever seen him eat is hamburgers and pizza.

Every time we stood together it was like a great game of compare and contrast. It's the age-old shtick of tall and short, fat and skinny, light and dark, serious and silly. We were just two sort of polar opposites—two bookends between which came some very interesting reading. He is extreme in his own right, but it's natural and normal to him. And I'm the same way, only with different extremes. Working together can be tough because we're both pretty set in our ways, yet somehow there's still a straight line that connects us. In my mind at least, Danger Mouse and I were two ships on our own seas that were somehow hearing the same exact signal in the distance on a lower frequency. Because deep down we shared directions, we didn't need to scream to be heard by one another.

Of course, sometimes Brian and I screamed anyway. For instance, we argued when I wanted to change the name of our group to Scarlet Fever because I liked the idea that we were these two very different characters who shared a rare sickness. I tried to get at the specific nature of our shared craziness in the song "Who Cares?" on the first Gnarls Barkley album, *St. Elsewhere*.

Basically, I'm complicated
I have a hard time taking the easy way
I wouldn't call it schizophrenia
But I'll be at least two people today

Anyone who's ever spent any time with me recognizes a lot of truth right there. At the time they were written, I thought those lyrics was just clever, but now they strikes me as downright poignant.

Still, while we were making that first album, "Crazy" was the one song that struck me hardest. We thought that it was the closest thing to a single we had. As the legend goes, I did my vocal for "Crazy" in one take. But I'm sure that many of the best and most important records of all time were done in one take. I'd bet Iggy Pop just had to sing "I Wanna Be Your Dog" one time.

"Crazy" wasn't just the title of our first and biggest hit—it was also our musical calling card to an entire universe of freaks and fellow travelers. Let me say this in case no one else ever does—the music of Gnarls Barkley was insanely strange and thus oddly universal. The song "Crazy" was a kind international declaration of the basic human right to be weird—a right I have been exercising religiously my whole life. But is it crazier to internalize whatever makes you different or insane or to be able to hogtie it and articulate it so that the whole world can sing and dance along with you?

People think that I'm crazy because I can talk about the utter insanity of the human condition and artfully explore that insanity for fun and profit. So there's a very thin line between being completely crazy and just being incredibly convinced and convincing too. That's what makes me a diehard and always has—whatever cause I was dying for at the time.

Essentially, succeeding in this world all comes down to being a very faithful person and I believe I've taken a quantum leap of faith—that's how I got here and that's how I've stayed here. I don't want to bore people with the math—I'd rather charm their pants off with the poetry of it all. If any of this sounds crazy to you, then good, I've done my job.

In the music business, it's feast or famine. "Crazy" became a moveable feast that sent me and Danger Mouse on a trip around the world. It took us to the Grammys together and just about everywhere music can go. I remember reading that "Crazy" was voted the biggest hit of the past decade. It was an anthem for outsiders everywhere that, at least for a time, made Danger Mouse and me insiders every-where in the world we went.

Still, the way that song was written and structured defied radio logic. The hook wasn't the same each time. It just appears the same, but it poses three different sets of circumstances. You should also notice that the only time I call myself crazy in the song is when I'm trying to call someone else crazy but acknowledging that I'm in no position to judge and criticize. We are all in no position to criticize because we're all trying to figure this life out with varying degrees of success. So I say, "You're crazy, just like me." What I'm trying to say there is "Let me take a little of the blame and we'll share it together"—that is, unless you don't want to be with me, because I'm on some whole other level. But I don't think we're on different levels because I'm standing here talking to you. You feel me? Maybe not, but that's my way of thinking.

When Danger Mouse later worked with Damon Albarn from Blur and the Gorillaz on their project *The Good, the Bad & the Queen*, Damon asked Danger Mouse, "So this song that you have with this guy CeeLo, who is he? I want to see him. What's he look like?" So Danger Mouse showed him a picture of me, and Damon said, "Oh damn, he's the real thing." Because he could immediately tell there was nothing pretty or pretentious about me. These eyes, they don't lie—and I'm not here on Earth to lie. I'm here to tell my truths. Everyone's been called crazy or felt crazy. And everyone has wanted to tell someone "Fuck You" a time or two.

Having a universal hit like "Crazy" opened a lot of doors for me, and it made me a very recognizable figure. And that's how I got to meet my childhood idol, Prince. I was hanging out with some friends in a club in Las Vegas. All of a sudden "Erotic City" started playing on the system—they must have cued it up when they saw Prince coming—then this beautiful woman walked in all alone, wearing a tight pencil skirt, horn-rimmed glasses, looking like a sexy stenographer. Just stunning, to say the least. Like some mermaid out of water. Then Prince walked in after her. He has this confident, swaggerish walk, and he blew right past us with the girl and his security guard. I saw he was looking at us, with a little smirk on his face, as they led him to this roped-off area. Next thing I knew, his security guard came over to say Prince wants to see me. So I went over there and sat down for a while. Out of everything he said, what I remembered the most was that he had listened to *St. Elsewhere*.

"Great album," he said. "It scared me, though."

I was like, "Well, *shiiiiit*... I don't know! Let me tell you how much you scared me when I was a kid!" So I told him about how when my mother was in that Pentecostal church they had a seminar warning us that Prince was up to demonic mischief when he released "Darling Nikki." Not only did the lyrics scare the hell out of us, but the backward part at the end of the song sounded like the devil himself. Actually, when you play the backward part forward, there was a positive message, and he was just being sly. But it didn't make no difference. "We were just terrified of you!" I told him. He laughed when I said that. We exchanged numbers and he ended up calling me, to say that he had been loving "Crazy." Years later I opened for him at Madison Square Garden and he played "Crazy" with me, one of the great moments of my life. If I could choose anyone to collaborate with on a musical project, Prince would be on top of my list.

I think Prince is the kind of weird we would all love to be. You could go crazy with that much talent in that little body. I don't even know what he's talking about half the time, but all of it means something to me. Prince is so cool. So calm and calming. So unlike some of my other collaborators.

As you can tell by now, Danger Mouse is dark—dark enough even to scare Prince. From my point of view, he's still in his dark night of the soul—or whatever he thinks he is doing. Seasons change and to me if you're just seeing the darkness, that means you're perpetuating that darkness. The world is always going to look dark if you're sitting in your room with all the shades down. Perpetuating the darkness is purposed. That's no mistake. That's a choice.

As time went on, I came to feel like I wanted to tell Danger Mouse, "You are not going to perpetuate the darkness on me, especially when the sun is out and I can see and feel it." See, I'm dark at night when the darkness feels right, but when the sun comes up, I see it and I get up and work and earn the day. That's how I feel about life—I earn the day and appreciate the opportunity that comes with it. That's me—I'm balanced just like the dusk and dawn, dawn and dusk. I felt I might lose that balance if I let Danger Mouse steer me into the underworld too often. And so I started leaning into the light and away from my dark companion.

By now there should be no confusion why we called our second Gnarls Barkley album *The Odd Couple.* In my opinion, our second album was better than the first, but

191

you don't get a second chance to make a first impression. And any way you looked at it, we had made a very big first impression. *St. Elsewhere* was one of those albums that entered the stratosphere and has never really left. The second album hit a kind of sophomore jinx because it was so close in terms of proximity to the original release. To me, Gnarls Barkley's second album is clearly just all-around better than the first album in every conceivable way, and probably in a few inconceivable ways too. *The Odd Couple* would be a killer coming out now, but like a lot of art and people I love, it was ahead of its time.

My biggest records have been psychological. I think that if I had stayed in school, I might have earned my masters in psychology, sociology, and maybe some other 'ologies too. Instead, music has given me some sanity and the most meaningful education of my life. I don't have a high school diploma. I have music—and it has educated me thoroughly. In music, I found my college, and my church too. Because I am so headstrong, and music is so personal and means so much to me, it is hard for me to be contained by any group for too long. Even one as willfully strange as Gnarls Barkley.

Once again in my creative life, I felt a familiar desire to move on. I felt like there was someone trying to hold me, or define me or tell me what I can or cannot do, and I just resented it. I think Danger Mouse's thing was to always protect the integrity of the project, so he didn't want anyone else to use me. I think he thought I was almost like a tortured little child, or someone's boy. Finally, I was like, stop. Enough. I am my own man.

Did I like Danger Mouse? Yeah, he's a funny guy and we had a lot of creative fun taking on the world together, and I hope we will again. But I will always demand R-E-S-P-E-C.T. This is still the music business, and I can be a team player, but I am a power forward on any team that has me. I will score. I will help you win. So if you want to assist me, then that's what you should be doing if you want to win too. Just don't stop me from playing my position and doing my thing. This is what so often breaks up teams, groups, and marriages.

If you want to be on my team, why would you assume I don't know my own position? I know I'm a strong power forward. I can't be the whole team, but I know what I'm doing on my court and I love doing it too. If I had been as quiet in front of the microphone as Danger Mouse was behind the keyboard, would Gnarls Barkley have had the same massive global impact? No way. For all of Brian's musical genius, I ended up having to sell a lot of Gnarls Barkley on my own personality because I'm pretty sure there wasn't anyone talking—or singing—but me.

Despite all of the tensions that were brewing, there was never a huge fight between us, and there still hasn't been. So I'm taking a note from Danger Mouse here because I know how honest he would be in his book, if and when he writes one. But eventually all of these tensions ate away at Gnarls Barkley as the duo. Personally, I like a little tension, but I think ultimately, Brian wanted even more control than I could give him or anybody. As I saw it, Danger Mouse became preoccupied with the perception of control. I feel like he got a little kick out of people thinking that he was Dr. Frankenstein and I was his performing monster. Hey, I suppose if that's what you get off on man, go for it. But I don't care about those kinds of games. In the end, I am nobody's monster but my own.

One of the upsides of tasting big success with Gnarls Barkley was that it brought me back together with Big Gipp and Goodie Mob in a big way. After years of just talking occasionally, our friendship began all over again. For all we'd been through since I stepped away from Goodie Mob, I always knew Gipp was my mutant brother in arms, and eventually, my brother came back into my life right when were both having a moment in the sun. It happened when we ran into each other backstage at the BMI Awards show in New York in 2006. I'll let Gipp fill you in on the details, but it led to a big thaw between me and the Mob. Before long we were back in each other's lives again, like brothers are meant to be.

Big Gipp: CeeLo and me had been talking the whole time during the Goodie Mob breakup, but no one else knew about it. Still, we really started getting our brotherhood back together at the BMI Awards. CeeLo had gotten a number 1 that year and so did I—Lo had "Crazy" with Gnarls Barkley go number 1 and I had "Grillz" by Nelly, which I was featured on, go to number 1 too. That night at the BMI Awards was first time we were in the room with our different crews, and when we saw each other across the room we attended to each other like we weren't even there with anybody. That was like our big reunion scene in this love story between two straight dudes. I remember CeeLo left Danger Mouse, and I left Nelly and that whole crew on the side. And we played around and joked around together like no time had passed at all. We both congratulated each other for being back on the top and for somehow getting there on our own crazy terms. And we both were in the same position. Lo was in a group, but Danger Mouse sort of ran that situation—or at least he thought he did. I was working with a group with Ali from St. Lunatics, but Nelly ran that situation. But still, one way or another, we had gotten back to number 1, and from that moment on, we were back in each other's lives too. That was a big moment for both of us. After that, the mood changed.

Goodie Mob showed up at a Gnarls Barkley show in Atlanta. Then when I was on the road with Nelly, and we had a show at the Tabernacle in Atlanta with Nelly and CeeLo came by to say hello. Nelly said to CeeLo, "Yo, Lo, you want to come up and perform tonight?" The other two Goodie Mobs guys were there and they were good to go. And CeeLo did it—and that was the first time we'd really gotten together onstage together in like years. That night was a great sensation. It was also CeeLo's chance to see the other possibilities of Goodie Mob being back together. Remember, this was not CeeLo's crowd or Goodie Mob's crowd—this was Nelly's crowd, and we won them over. We did "Black Ice" and "They Don't Dance No Mo," and that's when we first started testing the waters. So we started testing the waters again. We ended up doing twenty dates together, and that's when the campaign to do Goodie Mob really began. It was great to get to know each other again and see that we can still be friends and work together.

It was truly great to be hanging with the Mob again. For all the people you meet and work with in this business, it's important to surround yourself with those who you trust really have your back. Because if you think life gets easy when you taste a little success, please think again. In fact, finding my next big hit would be another long strange trip with, I confess, a very happy ending. For reasons that not even I can explain, we ended up spending basically three years and recording something like seventy songs to make my next album, *The Lady Killer*. Even if you are not already born crazy, which most of us are, the modern music business can definitely make you that way.

CHAPTER NINE

How to Make Friends and Influence People by Singing "Fuck You"

Yeah I'm sorry, I can't afford a Ferrari
But that don't mean I can't get you there.
I guess he's an Xbox and I'm more Atari,
But the way you play, your game ain't fair.

—*Christopher "Brody" Brown, Bruno Mars,*
CeeLo Green, Philip Lawrence, and Ari
Levine, "Fuck You"

TWO OF A KIND

*Making a little Grammy history with Gwyneth Paltrow in 2011
is a moment I will never forget. Aren't we pretty together?*

Photo by Kevin Mazur/WireImage

Even though Christine and I were divorced, we were still a family, and I still took my responsibilities to provide for her, Kingston, and the girls seriously. Yes, things got tough, but somehow we got through. For a while there wasn't always a lot of money in the bank, but there was food on the table. Still, I believed in myself—even if that was sometimes a minority opinion. A couple years of later, after "Crazy" came out and blew down any walls of resistance surrounding me, the same record company that didn't believe in me suddenly could not wait to get busy marketing me even though I wasn't with them anymore. They rushed into action and put together songs from those two solo albums and a couple Goodie Mob tracks and in 2009 released a kind of CeeLo's Greatest Non-Hits collection on me called *Closet Freak: The Best of Cee-Lo Green the Soul Machine*. I didn't like that. The label didn't see much worth in that music before I left, so why all the love now? The answer—as it usually is in the music business—is all about money.

What really ticked me off is that Arista didn't even ask me to go back and digitally remaster and improve things on the tracks. There were so many things I could have done better by then. I listen to old stuff and it sounds...old, because you're always working with the technology you had at the time. To me, the past is just a moment in time. I am infinitely more interested in the possibilities of *now*. Yes, I still remember almost everything that happened, but I don't like nostalgia for nostalgia's sake. This is because no matter what comes my way in this life, I am still my mother's son.

But in the end I have to thank Arista and all the record label executives who've tried to cajole me and control me over the years, because they became a big part of the inspiration for a charming little song that was about to make history.

_____

By 2010, I had already been a big part of some monster recordings known all around the world, but none of those tracks was a massive hit under my own name. So leave it to not so little me to finally make my own biggest and boldest impression yet by telling absolutely everyone in the world "Fuck You" and still having the world love me for it.

Despite what the song's lyrics might suggest, I wasn't just mad at any one girl. No, I was mad at a whole music business that in my mind had become way too contrived—more a destroyer of art instead of a platform for great artists. The way I saw it, the music business was getting increasingly soulless when great music should be all about soul. "Fuck You" was—for my part at least—a way of expressing blatant outright disrespect for the way things work in the music business and at the very same time getting paid loads of money for declaring that truth out loud.

In a much larger sense, "Fuck You" was another anthem that I put out into the stratosphere for all of life's underdogs. I was born an outsider, and the way I see it, I will never truly get on the inside. So even when things break my way, and I walk right up to the edge and stand surrounding the circumference of the inner circle looking in at all the beautiful people, I still know in my heart of hearts that I do not actually belong there.

To this very day, I feel like a lot of the powers that be in this world do not like me because I do not play by their rules and never have. So instead, I am the guy flipping the bird and shouting "Fuck You." In a million different ways in my life, I feel as if the music business has said to me, "We really don't understand people like you. You seem to have talent, but you don't fit into our picture." And time and time again, I try to explain to the beautiful people that whether they recognize it or not, we live in a world that is full of mutants. We who survive and overcome all obstacles even when we get dirty looks and don't get invited to the cool parties. The way that I see it, a singer like me only has two ways to get scratched by the masses: You can beg for attention or you can bite for it. Personally, I am a dog who is far too proud to beg.

———

So before "Fuck You," I just continued to stand my own ground and do my own thing. Having stepped away from Gnarls Barkley, I spent what felt like years trying to come up with the right record to get Atlantic excited about my next solo album. The music industry was changing dramatically now, and suddenly it seemed like the label was afraid to put anything out for fear that it might fail. As a true artist, I have never worked that way. In my heart, I am not interested in trying to blend in and just have a hit—any hit.

Big Gipp: The attitude of CeeLo's record company at the time was like "Okay, you're Mr. Gnarls Barkley, and you had that big hit, so here's your big record deal now give us another one of those 'Crazy' things." But CeeLo didn't have another "Crazy" in his back pocket, and that's not what he wanted to do anyway. So Atlantic was like "So maybe you do need Danger Mouse?" CeeLo's attitude as always was to stand his ground. He said, "No, I just need to do what I do." Lo was waiting on the right record as impactful as "Crazy," but just like that song, it had to be another great record that came totally out of left field. You just can't rush a classic. Like the Lord himself, CeeLo works in mysterious ways that work only for him. The man doesn't go by anyone else's guidelines or schedule. So for something like three years, it felt like CeeLo was making lots of records just for himself. CeeLo will wait on greatness, but record companies feel like time is money. But when record companies begin to doubt CeeLo, CeeLo just smiles more. He's very strategic that way. He just thinks it's funny when people underestimate him.

The weirdness for a moment or two between Bruno Mars and CeeLo only comes from the way the music business works today—or to be honest, kind of works today. There's a huge rush to come in and take credit for anything that works—because so little does work. There was some competition there because of that, but it's cool. We showed up in the studio and when we first came in they were like, "We have an idea for a song called 'Fuck You.'" They had that part. CeeLo walked outside and he said, "Gipp, I don't know if this shit will work. I can think of a million reasons and places it won't work, but I like it anyway. I told CeeLo, "This record is what a lot of people are going through. They're pissed and the bubble just burst and a lot of people are not happy. They're losing their homes. They're losing their jobs. And they're losing their relationships. I think this record could capture the core of what people are feeling out there right now." CeeLo said okay, and they started to change some words and flesh out the song. Lo got to the third verse and he just freestyled that whole "WHY" bit, and that was a turning point in his head. That's when he started to say, this record is funny. When they finished the record, I knew it was a smash—not as big a smash as it turned out to be, but I knew it was going to be plenty big. Because "Crazy" and "Fuck You" in my mind were kind of like great Goodie Mob records. It was CeeLo really saying something and going against the grain. There's a little bit of pop America that wants a taste of real life and not another song about partying in the club. But I think you needed a true messenger like CeeLo to deliver those kinds of left-field messages. No disrespect, but "Fuck You" would not have become what it became if it was sung by Bruno Mars or by anyone else in the solar system. There are songs only CeeLo could sell to the world. People believed CeeLo when he said, "Fuck You." He has to believe what he says and what he sings. He does not do this for the money—he does it because it's what he's here to do. And that's why he always wins, and as long as he keeps that attitude and that approach, I am betting that he keeps on winning.

But in the end—after all the industrial overthinking and music biz double-talk—it all usually comes down to one great song, that one undeniable song that explodes and leaves a mark that's powerful and permanent. "Fuck You" was—and is—one of those songs.

For the record, all our foul-mouthed fun began when our A&R man at Atlantic told me one day about a couple of staff writers who might be worth meeting. And that's how I was introduced to the very talented man the world now knows as Bruno Mars and his musical partner, Phil Lawrence. This is not to insult them—that's just who they were to me at that point because this was still early on in their journey. Today the Smeezingtons—Bruno, Phil, and their musical partner Ari Levine—are well-known and respected hit-makers, not just for Bruno himself but for lots others artists too, but back when we first met, their reputation was still just developing.

I was told that these young guys were very talented and that if I didn't mind, it would be good to open up a little creative space with them and bounce around some ideas. In this business, you meet a whole lot of people. Some professional relationships go nowhere fast—others will change your life—so it usually pays to keep an open mind. The word was that these would be good guys to get to know, and in this case at least, the word turned out to be right.

At the time, I was feeling creatively frustrated and open to trying anything different to get some different results. So Phil and Bruno came over to the place I was working, Nightbird Studios at the famous Sunset Marquis Hotel in LA. We all chatted for a while. I was working on a track at the time and they were being accommodating to me on this particular occasion and added some little background parts. Unfortunately, at some point that night, all the small talk became awkward for me, so I pulled the sort of disappearing act that I sometimes do when I get uncomfortable. I told Bruno and Phil that I was going to the restroom, and I just never came back.

So the chemistry wasn't exactly instant between us. In music as in love, you don't always experience love at first sight. Sometimes it takes a second coming. Eventually— despite my admittedly rude brush-off on our first writing date—we got back together, and the next time we really hit it off. It helped that these two guys Bruno Mars and Phil Lawrence turned out to be so much fun, and I have a fully functioning sense of humor too. As a result, the second time around, the three us talked and laughed and cracked jokes and got along like a trio of crazy frat brothers in a house on fire. And things suddenly became very productive.

People probably do not realize it, but "The Way You Are"—which later became a big smash for Bruno—was written for me. The song "Dr. Feelgood" that Travie McCoy ended up doing was my song initially too. And "The Other Side" that featured me with B.o.B. was originally going to be my song as well. So to their credit, these ambitious young guys were really pitching and trying to find something that truly fit me. I also learned that like most good artists, Bruno had already been through battles of his own. Like me, Bruno was an underdog with attitude who had to reinvent himself to make it big. Do you think it's easy for a little Filipino dude born Peter Gene Hernandez from Honolulu to take over the world? If so, think again. Even though Bruno was still a young dude, he'd already been through the ringer himself, including getting a record deal with Motown when he was only eighteen that ended in total frustration and with Bruno getting dropped. In the end, of course, talent wins out, and that would prove to be Motown's very big loss.

Over the three long years of recording material for what would become my *Lady Killer* album, I was—to put it nicely—extremely anxious to get the ball rolling with something. The core problem is that as an artist, I move quickly, and the music business doesn't move nearly as well as it used to do. I treasure being spontaneous, and the music business seems based on overthinking everything. It reminds me of those lines that I dramatically and rather sexily intone at the start of *The Lady Killer* album:

Hello there. My name is . . . not important.
I'm often asked what do I do for a living, and I respond
I do what I want. Spontaneity is the spice of life
And I've indulged quite a bit

Call me self-indulgent—hey, I've been called worse—but I think I understand the business of being CeeLo Green at least as well as anyone else on Earth. And it seemed pretty crazy to not take better advantage of all the global heat from the success of "Crazy," but in the music business today, record companies are remarkably reluctant to take a chance. They don't want to put anything but surefire hits out, and that kind of thinking can lead to a kind of musical paralysis.

They call what we do popular music, so in my mind you have got to bring the population into the equation eventually. The question always becomes—how are you going to know what people respond to about your music unless those people get the chance to hear your music? Especially in an age where technology has made music so easy to steal, it is protected from the public too much. For me, music is an art—not a science—and you need people to respond your art to really know how it works. As artists and executives, we all have ideas about what we think will work, but then the people ultimately tell us what they love. You've got to let people do their part. That being said, I didn't really get the support I was looking for, or at least that's how I felt. I was smiling through the pain, but I was still hurting and getting more and more tired waiting to make my next move.

As we were waiting for lighting to strike and Atlantic to finally put out a goddamn record, we continued to look for the exact right song that would light a fire under the record company's ass and kick-start the hearts of music lovers everywhere. That's an expensive process, so we started to work out of Bruno's home studio, and one day in particular, I went over and the guys were excited. Phil said, "We think we've got something. This could really be something." I loved their enthusiasm, but then again, by now, I knew they were highly excitable characters, so I said something like "Okay, what do you got?" And at this moment, what Bruno and Phil had was the start of a track. It was the first piano chords, no drums or anything, but it did have that cool "Bum-Bum-Bum" piano bit that the world would soon be grooving on.

Even then, the song was called "Fuck You," which at first sounded silly and by definition highly uncommercial. Thankfully, that was not the way we were thinking that day so we pushed on. To me, the concept of a song called "Fuck You" sounded just ridiculous enough to be spiteful—and just spiteful enough to be absolutely wonderful. What they first played me wasn't some runaway hit, or even a complete musical thought yet. Yet to my ears it was a very good, very rude start. So I immediately got into working on this song because it seemed even crazier than "Crazy," which meant this could finally be my chance to be totally absurd.

The secret of our success with "Fuck You" is that the storyline was fictitious, but the sentiment was genuine. Once we got into finishing the song, I connected with it in a big way. Like no shortage of recording artists before and after me, I wanted to tell the record company to go and fuck themselves in the sweetest possible way. And at least for a fleeting moment, I sincerely hoped that the song would be so rude that it would actually get me dropped by the label and I could get a fresh start.

But who would have guessed that after years of recording songs—a few of which I gave away on a mix tape and some good ones that no one will ever hear until I die and maybe not even then—my entire career as a recording artist would all come down to a song called "Fuck You"?

Talk about overnight sensations—that song literally took off in one day. We were leaving Los Angeles going to London and we had been given the word that our song was finally going to be released that day. And by the time we landed in London eight hours later, we heard that we had a massive hit record. They tell me that "Fuck You" was played more than two million times in the first five days.

Before we ever released "Fuck You," we cut the "clean"

version of the song known as "Forget You," thinking radio would want to jump onto the viral bandwagon without losing their licenses for playing something as flagrant and foul as the F word. Thankfully, all of our wishful thinking came true. We knew we had a hot flare of a first single, but we had a more politically correct and diplomatic version ready. Unlike most hit singles that drop off the charts pretty fast, this song just seemed to get bigger and bigger, staying on the Billboard Hot 100 for a total of forty-eight weeks, eventually knocking Lady Gaga off the number 1 position.

Bruno and Phil's idea for a song that literally said "Fuck You" to the listener spoke to my bad attitude. But somehow there was some kind of crazy sweetness to it. It felt like the whole world was singing along—whether it was Gwyneth Paltrow singing "Forget You" on *Glee* or appearing with me and some Muppets on the Grammy Awards. Hell, I know I will never forget seeing William Shatner doing "Fuck You" on George Lopez's talk show. Captain Kirk covering our dirty little ditty on national TV—how freaking cool is that? And now there's even a sweet young girl with a ukelele sitting in her messy bedroom and singing "Fuck You" on YouTube. And at last count, almost half a million people have watched it.

If "Fuck You" had bombed, no one would argue over it. But instead, there was a little bit of a credit grab because I think everybody was so proud of the song's success.

People often misunderstand what songwriting credits mean—and sometimes there are misunderstandings among co-writers too. So because there has been some confusion here, let me be clear here once and for all—I was definitely one of the writers of "Fuck You," and I'm fucking proud of it. When you produce music, you in a sense write it too, and the production of "Fuck You" is something Bruno deserves a lot of credit for—and the track sounded great. But just for the record, Phil Lawrence and I wrote most of the lyrics to "Fuck You," with Bruno throwing in lines as we thought out loud.

I'm trying to describe this diplomatically because originally I wasn't aware there was a tug-of-war over this song. But then I read interviews in which the guys seemed to be saying that they wrote the song, and I'm like god-damn, why would you say that? I don't know if someone told Bruno to claim that he wrote it for me to cause a little controversy and generate some press. But I know that he's a good guy and I don't think that reflects who he really is. In the end, there was no reason to take sides because we all shared this big victory together.

After bringing all that up about him, I want to give Bruno a compliment and say he is probably the best songwriter, singer, and producer of the young generation right now. He's got a great voice and amazing singles and people love him. Now, since I am eight years his senior, let's see where he is in another decade. I would not bet against him.

However we pulled it off, the fact is that "Fuck You"

is a brilliant record, and it's cool and even a little mind-blowing to have something that's an extension of you have such an impact. First of all, it's very flattering, humbling, and empowering too. For all the frustrations of this business and this life, hitting everyone like that for a moment in time gives you an awful lot of incentive to go on.

———

As soon as the single "Fuck You" hit big in August and September 2010, Atlantic could hardly wait to release *The Lady Killer* album in November.

Making *The Lady Killer* had been a whole other trip. Gnarls Barkley was a more cerebral and an unstable element—truly crazy stuff. This process was more stable and purposeful. My idea was that I would not so much make an album as a movie. From the title to the music to the packaging, I wanted to create my own musical spy film, something truly cinematic with edge and elegance that was inspired the great lady-killers of the past, from James Bond to Serge Gainsbourg to Barry White. That's the good thing for me—lady-killers come in all sizes and colors and ages. It's not about race or being another pretty face—it's about substance and style. Fortunately, for me and for all the ladies out there, I just so happen to have extra servings of both. Like James Bond, I was a ladies' man on a mission—a journey that took me through songs like "Bright Lights Bigger City" and "It's OK."

I can be my own toughest critic, and I will honestly

tell you that I am not sure that I ever got my "movie" *The Lady Killer* exactly right—maybe I'll do another director's cut one of these days. Generally I don't go out of my way to read reviews, but when I hear they're really good, I will make a happy exception. One review that I particularly enjoyed ran in *Rolling Stone,* in which Jody Rosen began his review like this:

> How can you not love CeeLo? He's a virtuoso rapper who has one of pop's most unique singing voices. He's a self-proclaimed lady-killer who's roughly as tall as a mini-refrigerator and as broad as a Hummer. He wears pink suits. He put a song called "Fuck You" in the Top 20. He is, in other words, an original: a showman with a penchant for scrambling a variety of sounds—rock, soul, hip-hop, spaghetti-Western soundtracks—into something deliciously strange. That weirdness makes CeeLo's first album since Gnarls Barkley blew up one of the most engrossing records of 2010.

How can you not love CeeLo? Thinking about it, that's the ultimate question I have been asking all of my mutant life.

CHAPTER TEN

The Voice in My Head and The Voice on the Screen

I am fighting for the liberation
Of voices with something to say
Like many before me
For glory, you'll have to stand
   in harm's way
I'm no savior, just a soldier, soldier
   with an order
So I have no choice but to trust in God
   cause it must be done
My only fear is what might have been,
   if I didn't fight to win.

     —*Goodie Mob, "Fight to Win"*

I RECOGNIZE THE CHAIR
From the start, I felt right at home on The Voice.
Here I am in a Misfits T-shirt during Season One.
Photo by Lewis Jacobs/NBC via Getty Images

In most every supernatural and epic journey, the hero survives his trials of fire and darkness and returns to the land of the living with new knowledge to share with the world. In my particular fable, the sweet elixir that I had gained from my trials and tribulations and triumphs was an understanding of how music is made and what it takes to be true to yourself and your vision as an artist. And what better way to share this knowledge than to coach a group of talented young singers, and do it in front of something like 12 million viewers each week?

I knew going in that *The Voice* had the potential to make some history, but I had no idea of the awesome impact the show would have on the fortunes of our network home NBC, on the world of TV generally—and more specifically on me and my crazy career. In retrospect, I think it is quite amazing that this all has happened on a show that's called *The Voice.*

If you remember, this thick slice of the high life called Lo that I have been serving up here began with a much younger and less confident version of me hearing some amazing voices in my head—voices that filled the void left by a father who could not be there. Through the enduring mystery of music, I heard those powerful and expressive voices of men who sang me all the lessons that my own father could not be around to teach me. As in some forgotten old Bible story set in the Dirty South, those voices in my head drove me to do things that I otherwise might never have dared. I thank God—and any other deities involved—that those beautiful voices ultimately won out over the voices around me telling me that my life didn't matter—that I was too strange, too odd looking, too flawed to ever win big. Instead, I listened to enough of those encouraging musical voices in my head and took enough of their lessons to heart that eventually I found my own voice. And with a little luck—or in my mind precisely according to plan—my own voice is now being heard all around this world. Against some long odds and despite people who told me I was an underdog who was just going to get whipped by life, my voice has connected with millions of people and traveled the world through musical statements like "Crazy" and "Fuck You."

On some level, I always felt fated to share my unique voice with the world, but sharing my face with the general public was a whole other thing. One of the amazing things about the past few years has been seeing my now-famous face plastered all over television and anywhere else people are looking. Part of me loves it. Part of me hates it. On the plus side of the fame equation, I can't help thinking about the possibility that somewhere out there, some young kid having a hard time or just feeling lonely is seeing me on

The Voice and hearing my words of encouragement and feeling them stir something inside him or her. And just as I did back when I was watching television for hours by myself growing up, that theoretical kid out there may be staring at me on the TV screen to try and figure out how to speak and how to behave. That kid might not have a dad, or might be an orphan, or just not feel loved or understood. I believe there are lots of misfits out there watching and looking for any helpful clues about this journey called life. The fact that my own crazy journey has taken me all the way from hearing voices in my head to hearing, judging, and nurturing voices for a living on *The Voice* is enough to leave me speechless—almost.

The big idea of putting me in one of those famous chairs on *The Voice* came from one of the biggest names in TV. Mark Burnett had already brought the world *Survivor*, and in show biz terms, who is more of a survivor than me? Okay, I may not have eaten a lot of bugs in my time, but I sure as hell have eaten my share of shit in the music business—and who's really to say which is more dangerous to your health?

When I asked him why he wanted me to be a part of *The Voice*, it was not my own remarkable survival instincts that made him interested in meeting me but rather my singular flair as a flamboyant showman. Those are Mark's words—not mine. He told me that he saw me perform with Gnarls Barkley and was immediately impressed, so much so that when he heard that I was appearing as a musical guest on *Saturday Night Live*, Mark said he actually went to the show. He wanted to see what I was like not only performing musically on the show, but also working my way into a few skits. Mark even asked *Saturday Night Live*'s producer Lorne Michaels what he thought of my skills, and thankfully Lorne gave me rave reviews.

I suppose that one great showman can recognize another. I liked Mark's spirit right away. It does not hurt that Mark—who is dangerously charming and pretty easy to talk to for a major TV tycoon—has definitely led his own decidedly colorful life. This is not a prince who was born into the royal family—he was the only child of two factory workers in England, a former paratrooper who jumped the pond and scratched out a living in Los Angeles before becoming a media power player.

The show had started in 2010 in the Netherlands as *The Voice of Holland created by John de Mol*, but it was too good a TV format to stay a Dutch TV treat forever, so Mark Burnett brought his own voice and vision to making the show into an American TV sensation. When Mark showed me the original Dutch show, I could immediately see that it could be very, very big on this side of the Atlantic.

I thought being on *The Voice* was a fascinating offer— but one that still scared me because in my mind, great artists are supposed to be a little mysterious and somewhat elusive. For instance, I sure couldn't imagine Prince being a regular on any TV show—so putting my face and my persona on TV constantly seemed a little uncomfortable.

TV is a large, enormous force compared to making music. The way people approach you and think that they know you is different in television because they experience you coming into their living room. I think that's part of the reason people feel celebrities should not have any zone of privacy today—because we go into your homes, you feel you have the right to get into my personal business too. That's just the price of fame for celebrities today. And for better and for worse, I have become a celebrity with all that entails these days.

I am just a mutant man and I know it. Yet I thought what I could do creatively on a show like *The Voice* was worth doing because it celebrates people—all kinds of people who are stars in their own night skies. I never got involved in this industry to revel in my own celebrity. I have been an outcast and alienated for far too long to do that. I would rather use all the attention to try to find some common ground. My feeling is that if you and I talked to one another for long enough, we would realize that we are both unique, both peculiar, both downright weird, and that eventually I would discover that you are likely just as crazy as me. For me, that realization takes the hurt off of being crazy.

Eventually, despite any skepticism or concerns about overexposure, I was sold on doing the show. My managers were excited about it too, but back then, some very powerful people on the record company side told us that this was not good idea at all.

Big Gipp: One of the most powerful men in the business, Lyor Cohen—who was the North American Chairman and CEO of Recorded Music for Warner Music Group back then—called a special meeting just to basically say "Lo, don't do it!" Lyor is a man who people usually listen to. But true to form, CeeLo was like "Oh, *don't* do it?" And immediately Lo decided he was doing it anyway. And of course, then *The Voice* went right through the roof.

The show worked because it was real, and CeeLo worked on *The Voice* because he's real too. He's seen the world and made history without getting a high school education. Despite coming from nothing, Lo's performed for the royals in England and hung with the President of the United States. He's a kid who was a street thug who now gets his ass kissed by network executives. You want to know why *The Voice* happened? For the same reason most of the good things in CeeLo's career have happened. It's not because he listened to the smartest guys in the room. It's not because he listened to the "conventional wisdom"—because he is way too unconventional for that shit. CeeLo won big because he went with his gut and he was right again. Lo turned out to be the perfect person for *The Voice* because he's a great singer and a student of great artists. He felt more confident because he was in business with a TV producer who comes from the grind—a self-made man like Mark Burnett. Diversity comes in all colors and races, and sometimes it even comes with a British accent.

Everybody jelled into a real family pretty quickly because right away it became clear that this show was going to be around for a while. I think what CeeLo has gotten out of it is a kind of discipline—he's become a better judge of vocal character, a better leader, and a better motivator of others. And to keep things real, it's also made Lo a shitload of money, and that's not a bad thing either. It's been a trip to watch Lo coach people because he's always done that and been a brainiac when it comes to knowing music history and putting that knowledge to use. If I was on *The Voice*, I'd want Lo to be my coach because that man does some real *sensei*-type shit. Lo picks songs on some deeper level. He knows how to put people in their element—and then he knows how to take them out of their element, because if they can work outside of their comfort zone, then they have a fighting chance to make their way in this business.

Fortunately, smarter voices prevailed. Like one of my managers, Larry Mestel. I met Larry back when he was on the label side and I recognized how smart he is. Now he's one of the guys who are trying to forge a new music business that really works. The old model was just about selling records, but today, the music business is less about hard product and more about branding yourself and working with other people to market your music and all that you do.

That's something I hope all these kids on all the talent shows today realize. A record deal was once the end-all, be-all mission, the dream destination. That was never completely true because the music business has always had a high failure rate. We forget that because just like war history is made by the victor, music history tends to get made by the biggest success stories.

When I finally decided to do the show, which first aired in April 2011, I thought of *The Voice* as being what I call "a token of tangibility"—a sort of bridge of understanding for anyone who perceived me as being a little elusive, ambiguous, and enigmatic. Personally, I consider all three of those words to be compliments, but I felt as though the time had come for me to step forward toward the general public and let them get a better sense of who I am. This way they will know that I'm not just some crazy-looking guy telling them all "Fuck You."

One of the biggest selling points for me was that the casting of the show was spectacular, with four people who all fit very different molds. This is one place where we succeeded where so many other talent shows failed. Mark Burnett knew that the people turning in those chairs on *The Voice* all should bring different flavors to our TV feast.

Blake Shelton is a good-looking good old country boy with a big heart of gold who everyone could relate to—including me as a country boy of a different shade. Blake and I hit it off right away.

Adam Levine is a rock and roll heartthrob with a lot of heart. When I was cutting *The Lady Killer* album, Adam's great band Maroon 5 was in the next studio, and we'd pass each other in the halls at all hours. We've become good buddies—which was great for me because Los Angeles, where we shoot *The Voice*, is his hometown and he's got it wired. Adam is a local kid made good who grew up with some privilege, but also with a lot of soul that comes across in those bedroom eyes the sexy ladies like to look into so much.

What can you say about Christina Aguilera? She is a true global superstar whose talent has been crystal clear since she was a kid and has only increased since she has lived a little and become the awesome woman she is today. When you're on a show called *The Voice*, it surely doesn't hurt to have one of the greatest voices in the world sitting beside you as a coach. Recently I recorded the famously sexy duet "Baby It's Cold Outside" with Christina for my *CeeLo's Magic Moment* Christmas album, and let me tell you firsthand, that lady is one hot duet partner and a formidable presence who can be sweet when she wants to be and a "Fighter" when she needs to be. I want to thank Christina for that sultry little Christmas gift to me.

Together, the four of us have made a pretty winning team. Despite having made a splash on a few award shows,

I'd had most of my experience in TV on the other side of the screen. Yet even I could tell that Mark knew how to build a television show to last—in part because he is so damn good at what he does and in part because that's where the money is in TV. So Mark surrounded us with an altogether excellent team, including our host Carson Daly—a true music guy who helps keep our show together when the coaches get out of control—which is more often than you might want to imagine. We've become like a little family on *The Voice*, and we don't just sit down together in the chairs. Off camera, there are card games outside the trailers, and some of us are practical jokers—as my homeboy Usher, a Season Four rookie, recently learned. You never know what might happen next.

Each of us coaches came from very different backgrounds, and all of us made pretty good names for ourselves, but I give you my word that at one time or another, all of us felt like underdogs, undervalued and written off. Somebody along the way told us that we could not do what we wanted to do. You don't go far in show business without someone telling you "No, you can't." And so yes, we did.

I have no regrets whatsoever about becoming a TV fixture in such a positive, musical, and fun way. I've loved the chance to work with so many talented young artists, from Nakia and Vicci Martinez back in Season One right through to Nicholas David and Trevin Hunte in Season Three. I have wonderful stories about each of my team members, but I don't want to leave some of them out by singling out any of them. In my mind, they are all stars.

I have to say that I'm always rooting for the underdog on *The Voice*, because I've always felt like an underdog myself. I guess you could say I've got a working-class-hero kind of quality to what I do. I love people whether they're as normal or abnormal as me, even if they consider me strange or different. Wait a minute! That's where the whole question in "Crazy" came from—hey, if you think *I'm* crazy, I think *you're* crazy!

However much of an oddball artist I am, I wanted the world to know that I am also a professional, and I take pride in being a professional. The fact that I get to do what I do for a living is not luck. I know what I am doing. My integrity is intact. The best lesson that I can teach the young artists who come on my teams is if you're truly talented and really fortunate, you can make a career out of being yourself artistically for the rest of your life. That's the dream. That's the ultimate achievement. So I encourage artists on the way up to go for gold. But in order to do that, you have to ask yourself a very big question: Who are you? If you want the whole world to know who you are, you better answer that question for yourself first.

If I ever really let others define me, I'd probably be locked up in a Georgia prison right now. Throughout my life I have never been comfortable with the idea of any other man or woman determining my fate. That is why I have always listened first and foremost to one voice—and that's the one that comes from deep within me.

Even with the mostly young artists I have worked with on *The Voice*, I always try to encourage them to listen not just to me but to their own hearts and souls. Do you think a timeless artist like Prince asked for a lot of advice on what kind of music to make? I surely don't think so. As I see it, Prince started a revolution because he made the music that he heard inside his own head and in his own heart. When I listen to a classic album like *Dirty Mind* or *1999* or *Purple Rain*, I hear a young Prince making the music that he had to make because he was expressing something burning deep inside himself. For my money, that's what music should be before it ever becomes a business—music should be a powerful form of personal expression.

Today, there are far too many artists—and that is using the term "artist" way too loosely—who take the opposite approach. They listen to every voice telling them what to do and what will sell. These kinds of wannabe artists try to play by the rules and they play it safe. They think that they can fake it and still make it. And maybe they can for a minute or even for fifteen minutes. But soon after that, their pop expiration date comes due.

In music and in life, my advice is to choose your battles and then fight your heart out for whatever you believe in. At least if you win that way, it will have been worth the battle.

Let it be said that despite being written off many times by people who underestimated me to be a loser, I have time and time again reacted instead like the winner I am. I have always reacted by consistently standing up for myself—especially when no one else would. Life is many things, but too often for too many of us underdogs, life can be a street fight. Fortunately, I was born a street fighter, and most of the times I have won my battles or, at the very least, I lived to fight another day.

Recently, Goodie Mob and I recorded a song called "Fight to Win," which we performed on *The Voice* in April 2012. We took the stage wearing gold uniforms like super-heroes, beautiful battle-scarred survivors bathed in light and glory, walking through smoke and ruins. While the audience roared and Adam, Blake, and Christina rocked in their seats, I swept my arm out to silently present my crew, blending my old world with my new one, coming full circle. T-Mo started rapping:

> *Fight to win, stand up straight*
> *No debate, pushed by hate, concentrate*
> *Penetrate, generate, motivate*
> *Live by faith, keep believing,*
> *I know the reason,*
> *It's the season, now's the time*
> *Keep on dreaming, keep on leading*
> *And keep on fighting*

In a way, that song is the story of my entire life. Fighting—whether it's with our fists or with our wits—is what we underdogs have always had to do in order to survive. We fight the good fight even when the odds are stacked against us. We fight for our lives. We fight to get friendship. We fight for love. And if we're really lucky, we fight to win and actually do triumph in the end. To some

I may look like a loser or a freak, but in my heart, I am a world-champion prizefighter, and until the day I die, I will always keep my eyes on the prize.

———————

The Season Three finale of *The Voice* was a little poignant for me, because I had decided to take a temporary break from the next season to in order to focus on my own music career for a while. And there was somebody I met during that last episode who moved me deeply. A good friend of mine was at a game at the high school football stadium in Avondale, Georgia, when he saw a kid in the stands who looked just like me. Actually he was like a mini-me, because Jordan Jackson is an achondroplastic dwarf, otherwise known as a little person, and even though he's in ninth grade, he's about the size of a five-year-old child. Hank took a picture of Jordan and sent it to me, and I couldn't believe the resemblance. When we saw some YouTube clips of him dancing, I decided to fly him out and work him into the season finale.

We met in my dressing room at *The Voice* and I could tell right away that this kid was special. He was witty and poised, and so naturally talented. "Whassup, my man!" I said. "Come on and sit with me and tell me how you learned to dance."

"Videos!" he said.

Jordan learned everything by watching movies like *Step Up* and *You Got Served* and imitating all the moves until he had them down perfect. It reminded me so much of myself as a kid, imitating those classic singers until I sounded just like them, none of it with any formal training. There was something else in Jordan that I could relate to, and that was always being looked at sideways by people because you're different. I wanted him to know that people found me peculiar too, and when I was such a small kid growing up and dressing in old-man's clothes, people sometimes thought I was a dwarf. I could relate to the feeling of isolation that comes with being different. But I don't have to spell it out for Jordan. He could just see by my example how it all can turn out—if you're true to yourself. Under that beautiful smile he may have some of that anger I felt, because he might not know how to make his difference work for him, what it means for his life. It takes time to figure that out, but he will.

Jordan was such a huge hit dancing to "Play that Funky Music" with me and Nicholas David on *The Voice* that I hired him to be part of the show I was putting together in Las Vegas. Now he's a professional and can see a future for himself, doing what he loves to do. And if someone tells him that he looks like CeeLo, you know then that's cool! 'Cause I ain't bad looking... I'm just peculiar! I don't have to tell him, I just show him.

Today I love being part of *The Voice* success story, and not just for the money. Being on the show hasn't just been a paycheck to me—though the paycheck is very sweet. It's been an education too. So when I decided to take a break from Season Four, it was because I didn't just want to talk about being a great artist—I wanted to keep pushing myself to live up to my own advice and *be* one.

CHAPTER ELEVEN

A Prodigal Son Comes Home and Atlanta Goes Green

Now listen
It's morning and the prodigal son is shinin'
I yawn and stretch and get dressed for
    some mountain climbin'
I wear it well but this is not by my designin'
The inevitable has impeccable timin'
And if you left it up to me I'd say never
Only God could've brought us back together
And all I say is I obey
You see, the family tree is tatted on my back
    forever
Uh, and I feel purpose
The salvation army is at your service
Act like you heard it
Cause uh, our only challenge is balance
But I believe that the will of God is perfect
Now let's go

    —Goodie Mob, "Is That You God?"

I, LOBERACE

Las Vegas gave me a chance to connect again with my inner showman.

Photography by Meeno

The first order of business after taking a break from *The Voice* was to finish up a comeback album with Goodie Mob. As far back as 2007, when we announced the Goodie Mob reunion, Gipp and Khujo and T-Mo and I had been throwing around ideas and laying down tracks here and there with the mind to coming out with another album. One thing after another held it up, but we kept accumulating material. After *The Lady Killer* and *The Voice* put me back on top as a solo artist, it was time to get serious. I wanted to show that we truly were Still Standing, like my brother Khujo on his bionic limb, rising from the ashes. A lot of us don't survive long, where we're coming from. But we've made it this far, and it's time for Goodie Mob to be back on top again. We wanted to make a record to instill some imagination back into the music business. And for us to remind the world of what hip-hop is all about.

I don't have to rap for a living, but hip-hop and rap music is my culture. When we do Goodie Mob, we don't just rap about random thoughts. It's got to be real, and be purposed. Anything I've ever done is about civil and social service. It's all about people. You have to understand, I've committed my career to outshine the dark that I had done. I'm forever in my community's debt that way.

"Fight to Win" was first record out of the chute, followed in May 2012 by an intensely personal song called "Is That You God?" It perfectly sums up our situation, our new knowledge of acceptance that comes from suffering and struggling for so long. It was a sort of manifesto about what really matters in this world. We show brotherhood, family, forgiveness, and obedience—because I'm always obedient to what my art tells me to do.

I don't want to get too spiritual on you, but I've said before that if you could envision what music looked like, that would be God. Sometimes singing that song with my brothers, as with so many gospel songs and spirituals from my childhood, I can also understand what God sounds like here on Earth.

―――――――

But since I have always looked at life as a combo platter of choices between Good and Evil, it is also perfectly in character for me to set up shop in a place known as Sin City.

One way of pushing myself as an artist recently has been living out one of my biggest dreams as a performer by putting together *CeeLo Green Is Loberace*—my very own splashy yet soulful Las Vegas residency at the Planet Hollywood Resort and Casino. My whole life, I have loved the idea not just of performing but of putting on a real, big theatrical show that captures my spirit in a way that I can't completely do at every concert. At most shows, you work the room. In a residency, you create the room to suit your personality, and Lord knows I have a big personality. Yes, I love to sing for people, but I also love the concept of shocking audiences with a bold rush of spectacle, sight, sound, color, creativity, and charisma. Doing all that within the economics of the entertainment business today is not too easy, but that's the moon I choose to shoot for, and I'm going to do that any chance that I get.

I created *Loberace* to be a musical journey, from the roots of soul to psychedelic funk, hip-hop, and beyond, with my eclectic tastes splashed all over the set and interpreted by a bevy of very sexy dancing girls. Hey, this is Las Vegas, baby—what would a show be without a little titillation? I love to surround myself with the things that I love, so Goody Mob appeared every night, all of us dressed in gold and white robes like members of the world's funkiest choir. Boy George, one of my earliest heroes, was also part of my act, doing his gender-bending androgynous thing to perfection. I also showcased V, a slinky, sinuous singer from South Central with a voice that can knock you off your feet. I was so impressed with her that I took her on in a management deal. And it's not just because she knows that bald is beautiful. And, as promised, we brought out Jordan Jackson and his mom—and hired a tutor to keep him up with his lessons. He danced every night in a top hat and tails—another showman in the making.

CeeLo Is Loberace is not only my tribute to great historic showman Liberace—whose piano I used with the Muppets on the Grammys—but also to the great showmen who I grew up loving and still love to this day. I learned by watching the greats, like Prince and Sir Elton John, and I hope people could see their influences in my act.

I will never forget when Elton invited me to one of his famous Oscar parties. When he first saw me, Elton grabbed me, kissed me on the forehead, and just stood there shaking his head at me like he knew just how naughty and nice I was. And to me that moment was like the ultimate compliment—it was like Sir Elton was formally accepting me into a very select and very crazy club of showmen who simply will not be stopped. As much as anyone on Earth, Elton John knows exactly how much nuttiness, balls, and bravery you need in order to take those big chances in this life. I am proud to say that I feel like Elton and I are cut from the same colorful cloth—though Elton's cut of the cloth is probably a little pricier.

Elton's husband, David Furnish, once told me a funny story. He and Elton were watching the 2011 Grammys at home, and Elton walked away for a minute—just as I appeared on stage in a sequined aviator cap and corona of feathers and started my performance of "Forget You" with the Muppets. All of a sudden his phone started vibrating all over the table with hundreds of emails and texts saying "HURRY WATCH THE GRAMMYS NOW! CEELO IS CHANNELING ELTON! CEELO IS CHANNELING ELTON!"

If you're going to channel someone, how cool for it to be someone like Elton John—because as we all know, there is no one else like Elton John. He is an original and he influenced me and countless others both to be better

showmen and to be our better selves with all of his chari-
table work. I would love to have the chance to work with
him someday.

One dynamic diva that I *did* get to perform with was
Madonna, who invited me to be on her Super Bowl halftime show in February 2012. Actually, the first time she
had reached out to me was six years earlier, when Gnarls
Barkley played Coachella. Madonna must have caught
our act. Her first contact was just a message on my hotel
phone, asking if I wanted to do something together some
time. I'll be honest with you, I was blown away. And my
first reaction was an erection. I started singing "Madonna
wants to do something!" But that wasn't it—I was just
excited. Although I would have gladly done it if that had
been the request. That was just her way of letting me know
she knew what was going on and what was hot. I didn't
hear from her again until "Fuck You" had become such a
monster hit, and I was a star on *The Voice*.

When I met her for the Super Bowl rehearsals, she
was intense. She definitely pushes herself to the limit and
tries to work to the point of perfection, but hey, man, who
couldn't learn from that kind of work ethic? I'm honored
to learn a thing or two from a queen, from an American
icon loved all around the world. I didn't try to act like I
knew it all, especially around someone like Madonna
who's got about twenty years of international success on
me. So I was thrilled to be her underling for a moment,

just to get a glimpse into what it takes for her to survive for so long at that pace and at that altitude.

In the end, she wasn't the type to push a lot of words of wisdom; we just talked a bit to take direction from her on how she wanted me to sing the song. But we joked around a lot. She teased me about not being late for the Super Bowl halftime, so I guess she had heard about my habits. She was kidding around, but she is a very serious professional. She told me, "Get it right."

"It's too much sexual tension, Madonna!" I said. "There's a more direct way to handle this."

She was playing hot potato with me, so we teased each other back and forth like that. I felt like she came prepared to give me a hard time and to play hard too.

Like I've said, I'm not easily impressed by much, and I try to take things in stride. But being part of that spectacle and singing with Madonna in front of 113 million people was mind-blowing, and probably the biggest moment in my professional career to date.

Equally mind-blowing to me was the chance to work as an actor on the remake of the movie *Sparkle*. Not only did I get to sing "I'm a Man" with a full head of Cold Wave hair in the beginning of the film—I also got to share the late great Whitney Houston's last movie with her. Like everyone else on Earth, I loved Whitney Houston—one of the greatest voices of all time.

I remembered how when Whitney came to my hometown of Atlanta in the nineties, the city was on fire. She was an exciting addition to this musical hotbed—and Whitney kicking it in our neighborhood with Bobby Brown was one of the reasons that LaFace Records felt like the center of the world at the time. Atlanta was a place she really loved back then. You got the sense that celebrity was weighing on her—she really wanted to be an average person and not this big idea of Whitney Houston. A lot of people came to see she was human then. And a lot of people came to see her flaws—which she had like all of us. But I'm here to say that she was a great lady. Whitney was one of the biggest stars in the world, but what she wanted most then was to be a normal person. Atlanta was a place she could escape New York and Los Angeles and just be Whitney.

Yes, Whitney Houston had her share of ups and downs after that—and maybe more downs than ups. But I can tell you that at the end, Whitney was still magic. Her star power never left her. I spoke with Whitney on the phone just two days prior to her death, after Gipp and I ran into a mutual friend who put me on the phone with her. She asked me if I had seen an edit of movie, and I hadn't yet, and Whitney said, "Well, you did such a great job, baby." She said she was proud of me. Finally, she told me that I was going to be one of the all-time greats one day. That meant the world to me, and it always will, because it was coming from a woman who defined greatness for millions of us all around the world who will love her forever.

I've always loved acting, and these days I'm getting to do more of it. It was a kick being the voice of Murray in

Hotel Transylvania. I got to play a version of myself along-side Gipp on the NBC drama *Parenthood,* and I thought I was very convincing. I also did a guest spot with Charlie Sheen on *Anger Management*—another topic I know something about. I'd like to pursue even more acting jobs, and that's something my exposure on *The Voice* has helped open up for me.

———————

My fame has brought me places I'd never imagined, from performing for British royalty to hanging with Barack and Michelle Obama. I've never been political in a conventional way, but when the President of the United States is an African American—a *real* African American in this case—well, that's saying something about what all of us can achieve in this country. It's something to stand up and acknowledge. So I've supported Obama and performed at campaign fundraisers for him.

The last one I attended was held at Tyler Perry's studios on the West Side of Atlanta, near Greenbriar Mall. I drove over there with my sister, Shedonna, and a young niece and nephew who wanted to see the President. The route took us right past the mall, literally the scene of my youthful crimes. It was a surreal moment. I turned to Shedonna and pointed out a familiar bus stop. "Twenty years ago I stole a pair of tennis shoes from a kid right at that bus stop," I told her. "And now I'm going to perform for the President." At that moment I had to fall into prayer, thanking God for how far I had come in this world.

But when we got to the studio, I quickly returned to my usual self, acting almost on autopilot as I took the stage in front of a thousand people who were waiting for Obama to speak. As the band started striking some familiar chords, I asked, "Can I curse in here?" and then answered my own question as I launched into the opening verse of "Fuck You." I can't say that the room stood still. In fact, everybody was still dancing, but I could sense the oxygen suddenly sucked out of the air and I realized I had made a serious mistake. I quickly switched to the family-friendly version of the song, but the damage had been done in front of a whole lot of cameras.

After the show they led me back to the secure area where Shedonna and the kids were waiting. I was sweating bullets, and I didn't want to go back to meet the President. "I think I did a bad thing," I told my sister.

"Oh, don't worry about it," said Shedonna. "Let's go."

President Obama made a fuss about my niece and nephew, and they were thrilled. When it came time for us to shake hands, he never mentioned the song. All I can remember him saying is "Where's the cat?" Purrfect upstages me every time, even when she's not there. Then a campaign photographer took a picture of me with the President. For some reason, they never sent me a copy.

Word about the "Fuck You" incident spread fast. Certainly Fox News had fun with it later that night. And my grandmother was beside herself when she heard. She thought I had ruined my career. Shedonna called me that weekend and said, "Lo, Grandma's called an emergency prayer meeting with her Bible study group for you cursing in front of the President! Would you please call and tell her you're okay!" We assured her that the media had blown things out of proportion. It was bad, but not *that* bad. And my career has managed to survive my presidential *faux pas*.

The fame *The Voice* brought to me has also helped me to live out some of my other dreams. For instance, I want to become more of a businessman—and now I am co-owner of TY KU sake—which in my experience is not only a good product but also an effective aphrodisiac.

I love it now when my son Kingston sees me working on business projects so that he understands the hard work that goes into getting ahead. As I write this, he's becoming a young man, nearly a teenager. I'm an artist, so as a parent I'm definitely liberal as far as the law will allow. But I am also the law along with the liberty. In all things you should aspire for balance, especially with a child.

I'm not sure what Kingston wants to be when he grows up. He's inherited my ability to imitate sounds and voices. I was able to do that pretty well at his age. He can definitely sing, but he doesn't necessarily want to be a singer. I don't know where he's heading, but I know I'll always be there for him. At this age, he's already had nine more years of his father than I ever had, and that's an advantage. I'm hoping as he gets a little older, he'll be even more connected with me, we can do a lot more together. He wouldn't ever be in my way. I love him.

I remember when people ran to avoid me, and now they run to shake my hand or get my autograph. Yet I am the same man. How can I explain that? Well, I am pretty sure that somewhere deep inside of my chest cavity, it's painted that I was here before. That sounds artful, but here's the bottom line: I was fated to write an entirely different life for myself. Being normal was not an option, so I had to become extraordinary.

I feel like the love that I'm getting now is a reciprocation of an even deeper, deeper love. I don't think I've ever had the chance to say out loud how much I'm in love with what I do and the opportunity I've been given. In fact, today is probably the lightest my life has ever been. I feel young now, younger than when I was a child and things were so heavy. My journey started off uphill and eventually leveled off. I suppose some people get their toys early—and others like me just have to earn and enjoy them a little later.

It's pretty miraculous how many different people like what I do and are into it so intimately. It's gotten to the point where I'm not merely entertaining people anymore—I'm getting up under their skin in some other kind of way.

I hear from people all the time now who tell me that I give them hope that someone can be different and still be loved and appreciated on their own terms. Recently I was given an amazing photo book from Chicago of these challenged kids who were modeling and owning whatever physical issues they were dealing with—like missing limbs and others things that used to be called physical defects. It was very moving to see. I may not be that different, but somehow I represent those kids in the world today. I wonder sometimes if I appear deformed to people. That is not how I see myself. Personally, I think the truth is that I look like most people in the world—an actual human being with beautiful flaws.

Beneath the surface, we all have our broken places, and they help make us who we are. My life is a testament that if you really want to, you can turn pain not just into gold but also into joy to the world. We all know that the truest measure of wealth is not what we receive but what we give. And so I've started to give back to the community that gave me so much.

On a hot August day in 2012 I found myself right back where it all started for me in Atlanta, Georgia. My beautiful sister, Shedonna Alexander, and I were attending a groundbreaking ceremony for a greenhouse at the Southwest Atlanta Christian Academy—a place where I had caused no small amount of trouble as a child. But now I was back as co-founder, with my sister, of the nonprofit GreenHouse Foundation, which is dedicated to giving disadvantaged children access to "green" educations—and what better mission for a man who named himself "Green"? Shedonna runs the organization, which puts up greenhouses in underserved schools all over Atlanta so that kids can learn to grow their own food and take care of their environment. Basically, we're going to do our best to try to help make the

Dirty South and our world a little cleaner, and we're starting with kids because that's how we all start.

Shedonna and I were motivated to try to fill the
big shoes of two strong ladies who made our journeys
possible—our late mother, Sheila Callaway Tyler, and our
grandmother, Ruby Callaway Robinson, both of whom
showed us the importance of community service in their
own lives. This first greenhouse was dedicated in our
mother's name, and the Atlanta fire department presented
us with a plaque in her honor. We knew that she was there
in spirit that day. And thankfully, our grandmother, who
had been sick for a while, surprised me and showed up in
person. Seeing her out and about made me happier than
any hit record ever could.

The mayor of Atlanta came for the groundbreaking, and
so did Gipp, T-Mo, and Khujo. When I spoke to the crowd,
I spoke from the heart, even though I was reading from
my BlackBerry. "What a fantastic feeling to see so many
familiar faces," I said. "I hope I've made you laugh. I hope
I've made you cry. I hope I've made you think. I hope I've
made you wonder. I also hope that I am encouraging you
today... It's not just a thought, it's an action."

That's why I wrote this book. To encourage you, whoever
you are, however much a mutant you feel like, to take the
actions to make your dreams come true. Dreaming came

naturally to me because the voices inside my head early on ushered me into a world of possibility. In my life, I had to get the common sense to listen to the right voices. That's why on my right wrist I have a tattoo that says "Think." And on my left wrist I have another tattoo that says "Twice."

So until we meet again, I ask you to think twice, but dream big. That's because whether the world recognizes it yet or not, there's something beautiful in your voice, and you are and will always be the only one on Earth who can sing your song.

I promise passion! It pleases me to please the people I'm partial to. If time permits, I'm in two places at one time. Pieces of mind pulse with persistence, penetration. I can't seem to pick. I want partners, not employees. Two beauties have become business professionals who have taken me personally...So is the prospect of polygamy possible? As long as I don't have to divorce the idea, we have a deal. Thoughts?

ACKNOWLEDGMENTS

My life isn't over yet, but this book is.

So a loud "fuck you" to everyone who ever doubted that I would get this far. And an even louder "thank you" to everyone who helped me get this far, including my son, Kingston; my grandmother Ruby; my entire family; my brothers Big Gipp, Khujo, and T-Mo; Larry Mestel and my whole winning team at Primary Wave; Mark Burnett, NBC, and *The Voice* family; the tireless Meredith Smith and the whole team at the Creative Trust Literary Group; our brilliant editor Beth de Guzman and everyone at Grand Central Publishing; David Wild; and all of you out there in the world who took the time to buy and actually read my book. Thanks for sharing the Lo life for a while.

I will tell you this…the story isn't over, there's a lot more to come. Prepare for the next chapter of Lo!

PERMISSIONS

All rights for Roc Nation Music and Music Famamanem administered by EMI April Music Inc. All rights for Late 80's Music controlled and administered by Westside Independent Music Publishing, LLC. All rights for Thou Art the Hunger controlled and administered by Northside Independent Music Publishing, LLC. All rights reserved. Used by permission. Reprinted with permission of Hal Leonard Corporation.

"Dope Fiend Beat"
Words and music by Todd Shaw. Copyright © 1989 Universal Music–Z Songs and Srand Music. All rights controlled and administered by Universal Music–Z Songs. All rights reserved. Used by permission. Reprinted with permission of Hal Leonard Corporation.

"I Didn't Ask to Come"
Words and music by Patrick Brown, Raymon Murray, Rico Wade, Brandon Bennett, Robert Barnett, Thomas Burton, Cameron Gipp, Willie Knighton, Frederick Bell, and Antwan Patton. Copyright © 1995 Organized Noize Music (BMI), Hitco Music (BMI), EMI April Music Inc. (ASCAP), Big Sexy Music (ASCAP), Brown Branches and Green Bottles Music (BMI), Mutant Mindframe Music (BMI), T Mo 2 Music (BMI), and God Given Music (BMI). All rights for Organized Noize Music and Hitco Music administered by Bug Music, Inc., a BMG Chrysalis company. All rights for Big Sexy Music administered by EMI April Music Inc. All rights for Brown Branches and Green Bottles Music, Mutant Mindframe Music, and T Mo 2 Music administered by Primary Wave Music Publishing LLC. All rights reserved. Used by permission. Reprinted with permission of Hal Leonard Corporation.

"Free "
Words and music by Patrick Brown, Raymon Murray, Rico Wade, and Thomas Callaway. Copyright © 1995 Organized Noize Music (BMI), Hitco Music, (BMI) and God Given Music (BMI). All rights for Organized Noize Music and Hitco Music administered by Bug Music, Inc., a BMG Chrysalis company. All rights reserved. Used by permission.

"Guess Who"
Words and music by Robert Barnett, Thomas Burton, Cameron Gipp, and Willie Knighton. Copyright © 1995 Organized Noize Music (BMI), Hitco Music (BMI),

Brown Branches and Green Bottles Music (BMI), Mutant Mindframe Music (BMI), T Mo 2 Music (BMI), and God Given Music (BMI). All rights for Organized Noize Music and Hitco Music administered by Bug Music, Inc., a BMG Chrysalis company. All rights for Brown Branches and Green Bottles Music, Mutant Mindframe Music, and T Mo 2 Music administered by Primary Wave Music Publishing LLC. All rights reserved. Used by permission.

"Is That You God"
Words and Music by Thomas Callaway. Copyright © 2012 Chrysalis Songs, God Given Music (BMI). All rights for Chrysalis Songs and God Given Music administered by Chrysalis Music Group Inc., a BMG Chrysalis company. All rights reserved. Used by permission. Reprinted with permission of Hal Leonard Corporation.

"Beautiful Skin"
Words and music by Robert Barnett, Thomas Burton, Cameron Gipp, Willie Knighton, and Craig Love. Copyright © 1998 Chrysalis Songs, Goodie Mo'b Music Inc, EMI Blackwood Music, Inc., Swizole Music, and C'amore Music. All rights for Chrysalis Songs and Goodie Mo'b Music Inc. administered by Chrysalis Music Group Inc., a BMG Chrysalis company. All rights for Swizole Music and C'amore Music controlled and administered by EMI Blackwood Music Inc. All rights reserved. Used by permission. Reprinted with permission of Hal Leonard Corporation.

"Fight To Win"
Words and music by Thomas Callaway, Mike Hartnett, Robert Barnett, Cameron Gipp, and Willie Knighton. Copyright © 2012 Chrysalis Songs, God Given Music (BMI), Mike Hartnett Music Publishing, Elijahwins (BMI), Zagga Music (BMI), Joog Central Publishing (BMI), and Panache Publishing Unlimited (BMI). All rights for Chrysalis Songs and God Given Music administered by Chrysalis Music Group Inc., a BMG Chrysalis company. All rights for Mike Hartnett Music Publishing administered by Songs of Kobalt Music Publishing. All rights for Elijahwins, Zagga Music, Joog Central Publishing, and Panache Publishing Unlimited administered by Primary Wave Music Publishing LLC. All rights reserved. Used by permission. Reprinted with permission of Hal Leonard Corporation.

INDEX

Note: Page numbers in *italics* indicate photos.